DRAWING BASICS.

Genius Cat Books

 Genius Cat Books

www.geniuscatbooks.com
Parkland, FL

ABOUT THIS BOOK
The art for this book was created with photoshop and illustrator, using a Wacom Cintiq. Text was set in American Typewriter and Populaire. It was designed by Germán Blanco.

Copyright © 2023 Genius Cat Books.
All rights reserved. No part of this publication may be reproduced or distributed in any form or by any means without prior written consent from publisher.
ISBN: 978-1-938447-88-4
First edition, 2023

Our books may be purchased in bulk for promotional, educational, or business use. For more information, or to schedule an event, please visit
www.geniuscatbooks.com.

DRAWING BASICS.

This book belongs to:

Delahey

INTRO

OK, SO YOU WANT TO DRAW SOME <u>SILLY ANIMALS!</u>

ALL YOU NEED ARE SOME PENCILS AND YOUR IMAGINATION!

THIS BOOK IS FILLED WITH SILLY CHARACTERS FOR YOU TO LEARN HOW TO DRAW. YOU WILL ALSO LEARN FUN FACTS AND HOPEFULLY LEVEL UP YOUR DRAWING GAME WITH SOME TIPS AND TRICKS.

THIS BOOK IS FOR ALL LEVELS OF ARTIST SO DON'T FEEL INTIMIDATED, JUST PICK UP A PENCIL AND HAVE <u>FUN</u>!

Be on the look out for:

LEVEL UP!

This book will teach you step-by-step basics on how to draw silly characters but will also give you the chance to level up your drawings with some fun challenges!

DID YOU KNOW?

Whenever you see this header, you will learn some fun new facts about the animals you're learning to draw.

TIPS & TRICKS

The only way to learn how to draw is through practice, and the only way to get better is...more practice! These tips and tricks will help you improve by providing different ways to practice drawing.

Drawing Tools

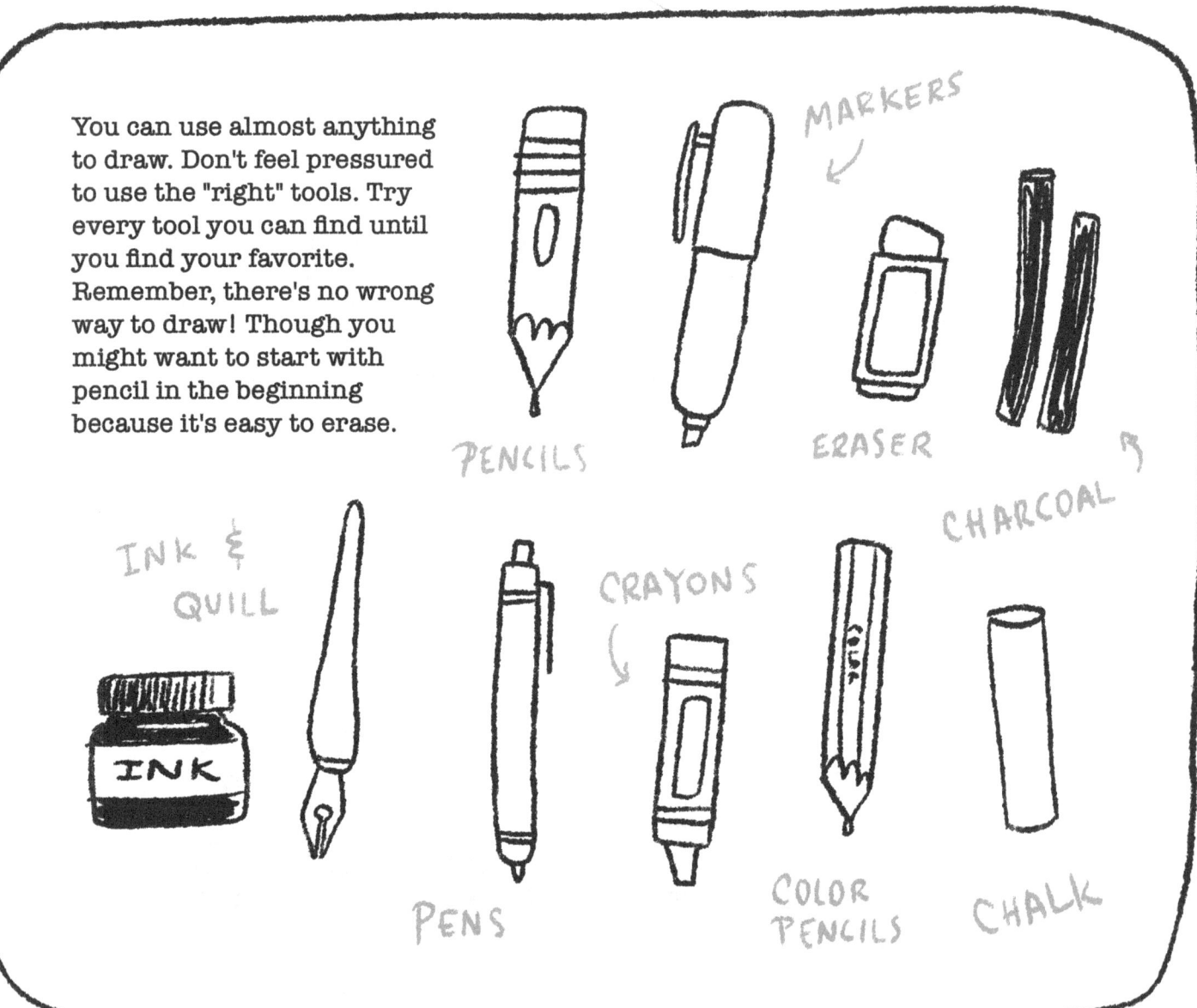

You can use almost anything to draw. Don't feel pressured to use the "right" tools. Try every tool you can find until you find your favorite. Remember, there's no wrong way to draw! Though you might want to start with pencil in the beginning because it's easy to erase.

TABLE OF CONTENTS

Drawing Basics

ROAM & ROAR 10

CHIRP & SOAR 32

BUZZ & CRAWL 54

HOP & SLITHER 76

SPLASH & SWIM 96

BARK & MEOW 118

ROAM & ROAR

Learn how to draw these silly animals!

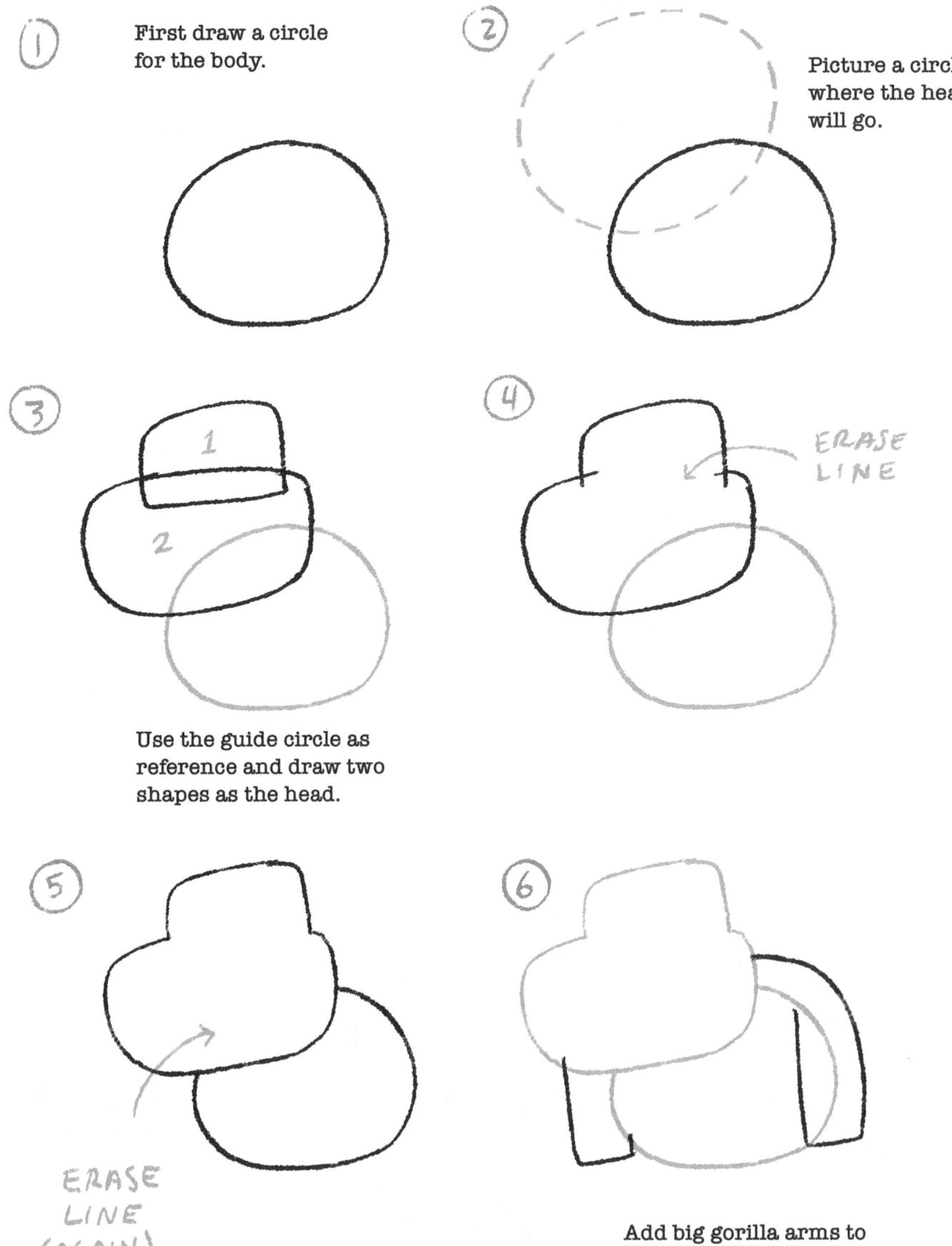

Erase the extra lines.

For the face, make an outline inside the head as shown and then erase the extra lines.

Add the legs and the chest.

Add the ears and the fur on top of the head.

Make squiggily lines to represent fur.

Draw a silly face and add the hands and feet.

Now you can draw a gorilla!

USE THE GRID TO COPY THE FIGURE

USE THE GRID TO COPY THE FIGURE

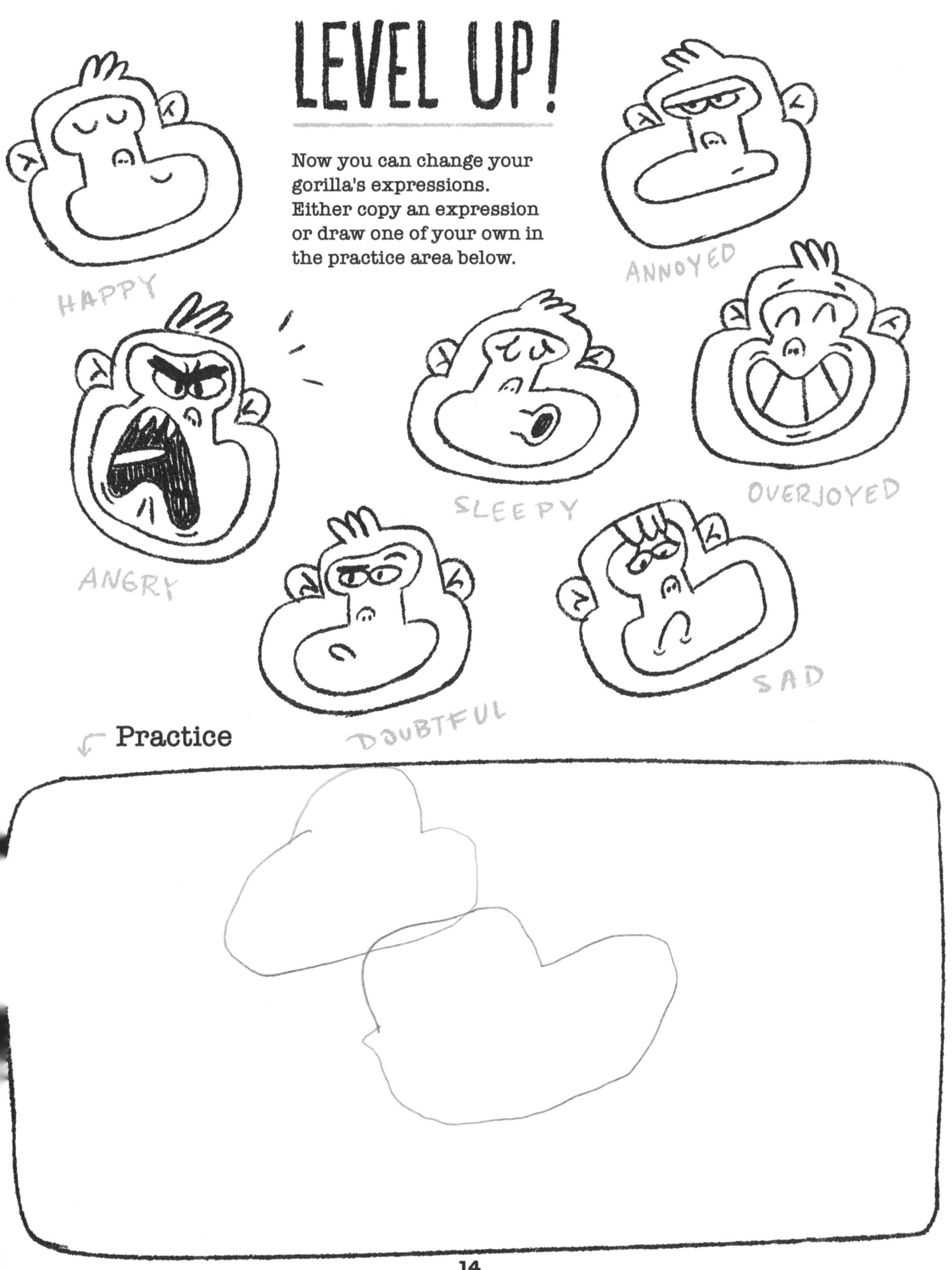

Giraffe

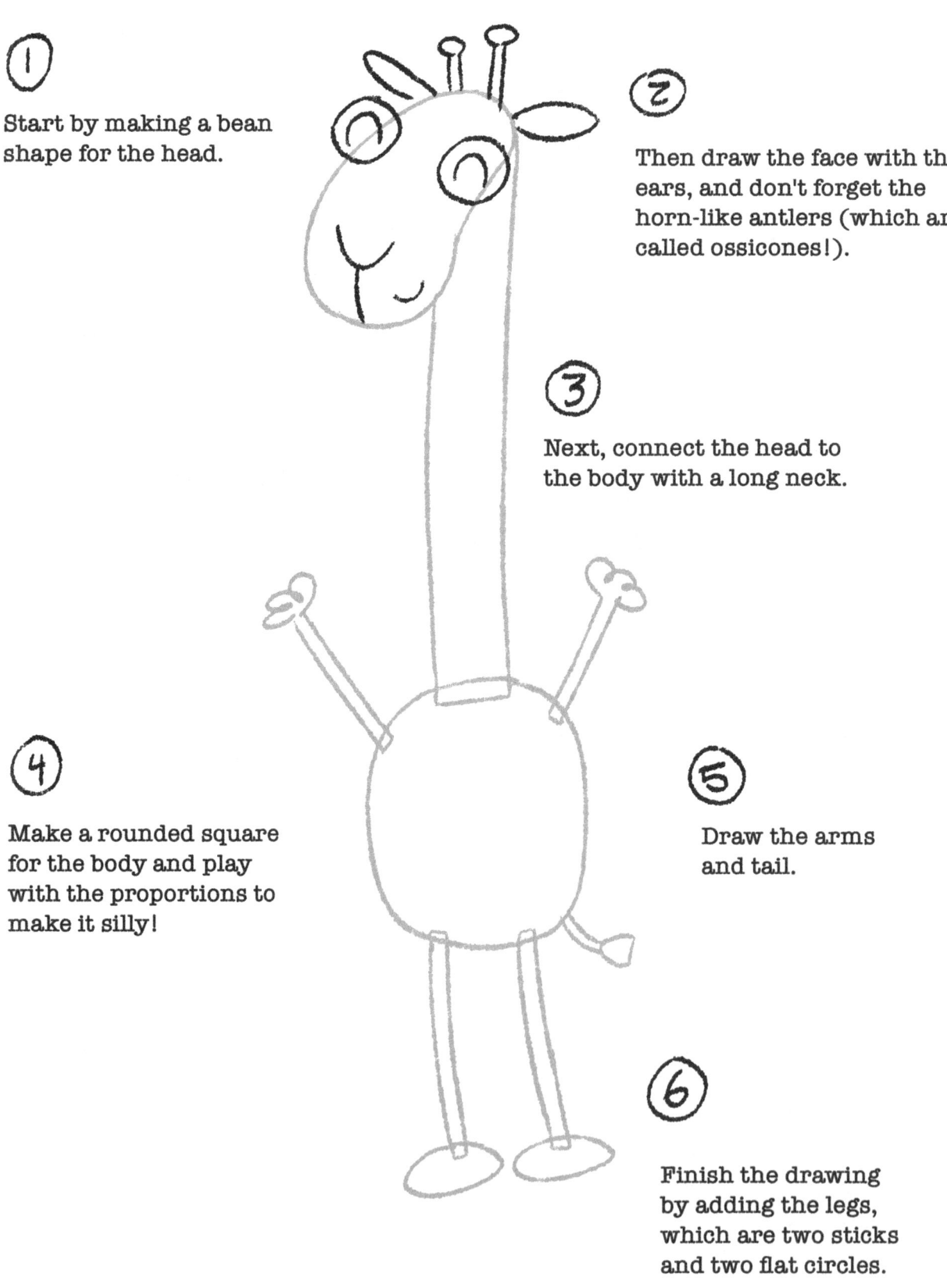

① Start by making a bean shape for the head.

② Then draw the face with the ears, and don't forget the horn-like antlers (which are called ossicones!).

③ Next, connect the head to the body with a long neck.

④ Make a rounded square for the body and play with the proportions to make it silly!

⑤ Draw the arms and tail.

⑥ Finish the drawing by adding the legs, which are two sticks and two flat circles.

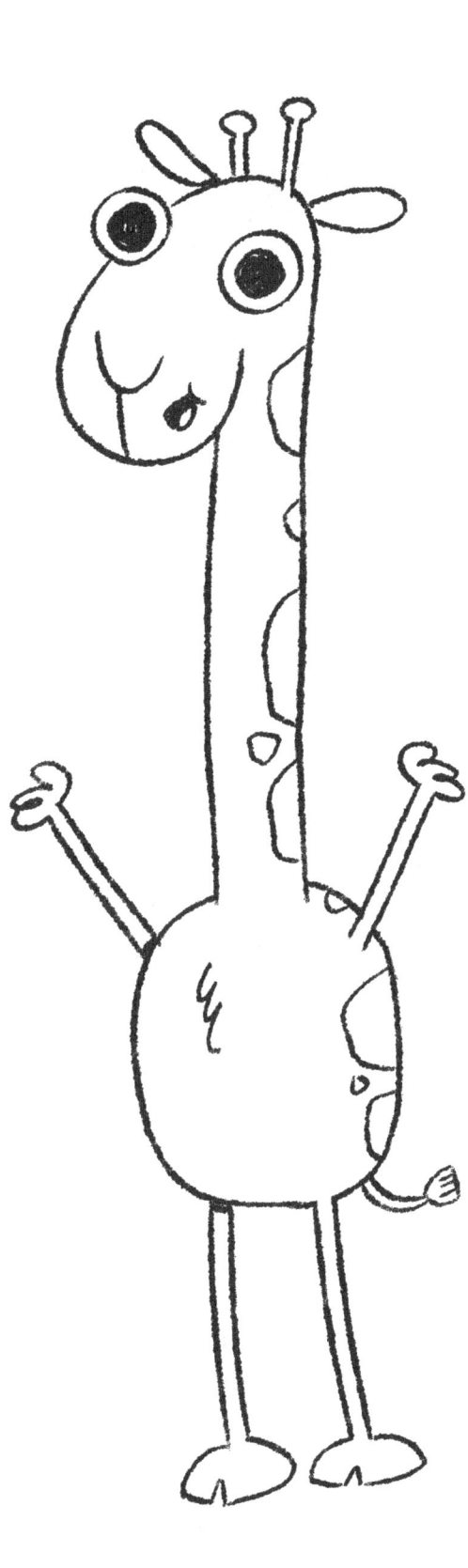

Practice the steps you learned to make your own giraffe.

Practice

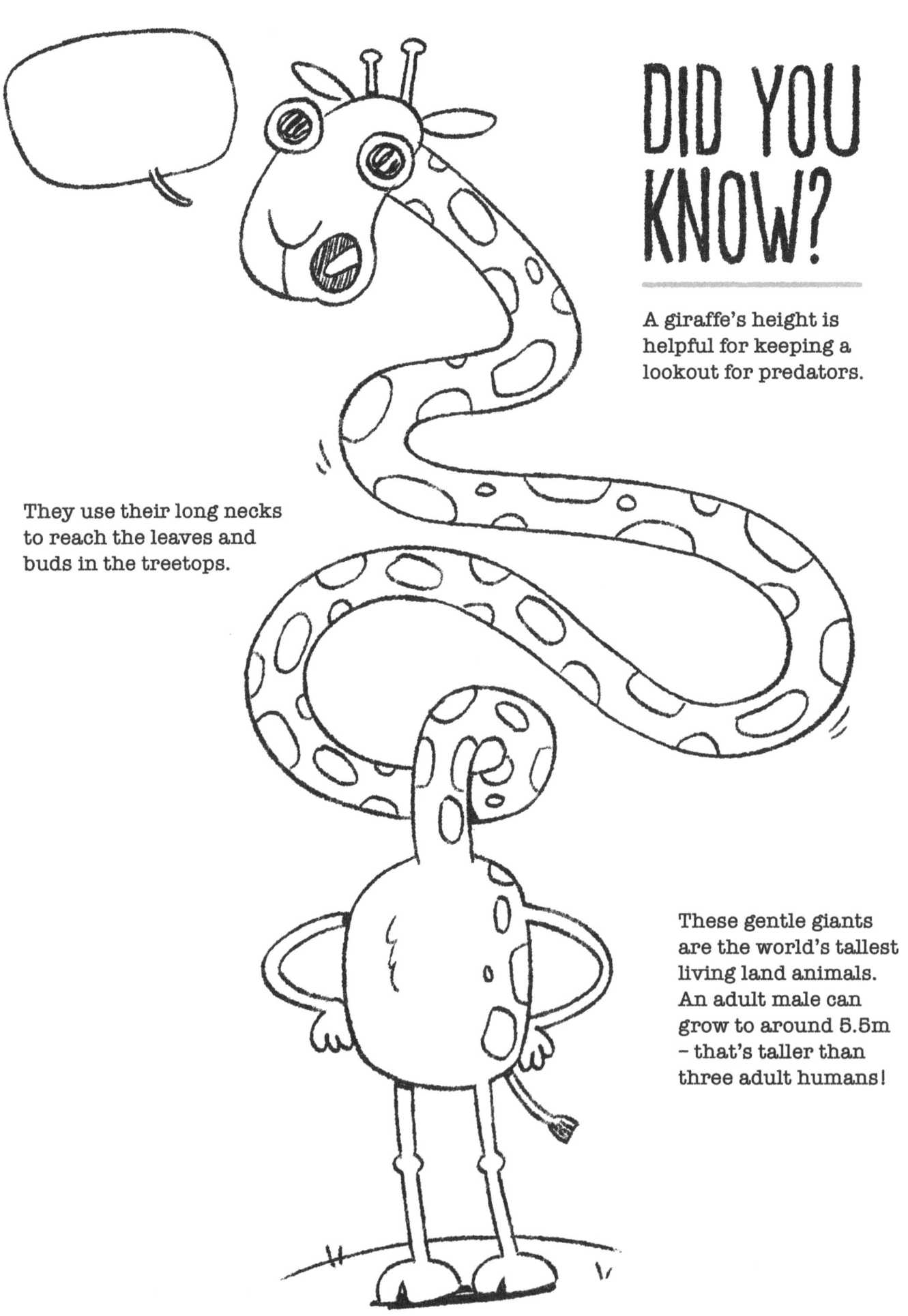

DID YOU KNOW?

A giraffe's height is helpful for keeping a lookout for predators.

They use their long necks to reach the leaves and buds in the treetops.

These gentle giants are the world's tallest living land animals. An adult male can grow to around 5.5m – that's taller than three adult humans!

Give the giraffe a fun neck.

Connect the head to the body by drawing the neck, but don't forget to have fun!

18

Rhino

Make the head - think of two hills connected at the bottom, or a wide heart!

Make the body a fun shape like a gumdrop.

Add the legs.

After you draw the legs, add the arms and give your rhino a fun expression.

This is a surprised rhino!

Practice

LEVEL UP!

Clothing

Use the rhino templates to practice dressing up your characters to achieve maximum silliness.

Practice

Use your imagination, and here are some examples if you need help!

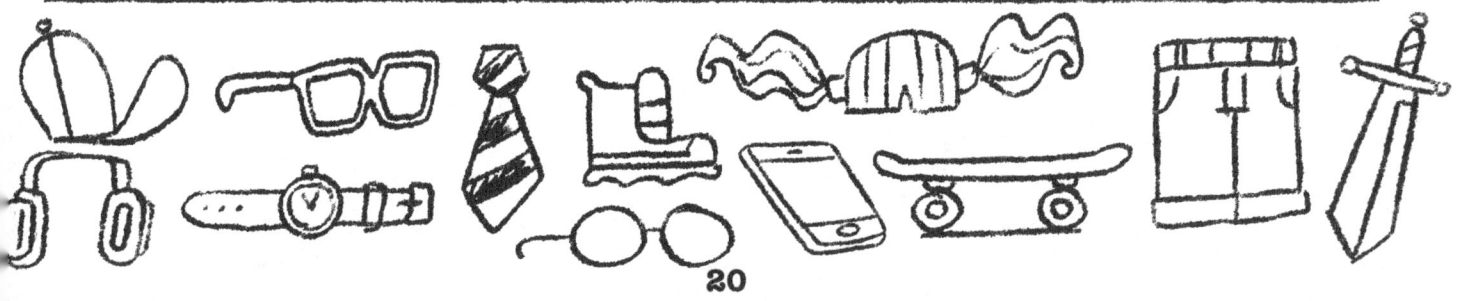

Lion

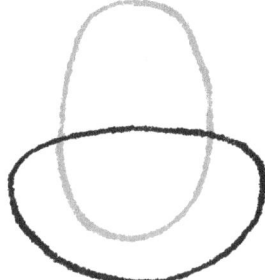

DID YOU KNOW?

The lion is the second largest cat in the world, followed by the tiger.

A lion may sleep up to 20 hours a day.

A lion's mane reveals a lot about his age. The darker the mane, the older the lion!

You can see how you can draw a lion by using simple shapes!

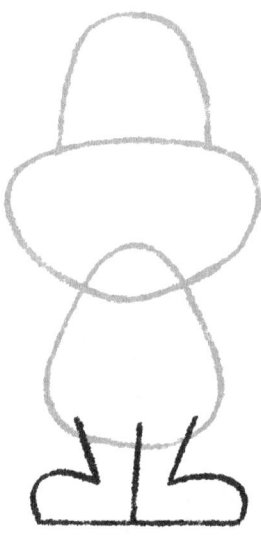

Add the legs.

Draw a fun mane. Give it a silly look.

WHO IS RUNNING AWAY FROM THE LION?

Draw some of the animals you learned here.

Zebra

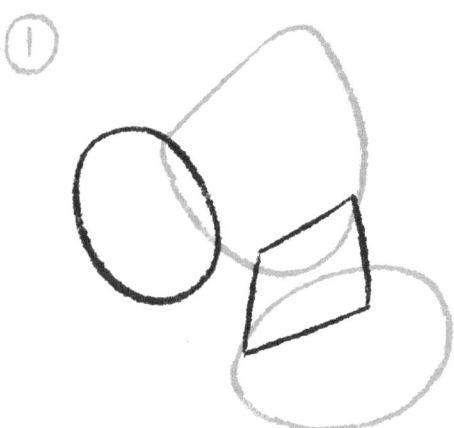

Start with simple shapes that stacked together form the body of the zebra.

Draw the mane and give the zebra legs. Next, add the arms and the face.

REFINE →

Once you finished outlining the basic shape, remember to give it your personal touch when adding the final details!

Elephant

Once you learn to draw the elephant, try new and more expresive positions, such as the elephant walking or dancing.

LEVEL UP!

It's always fun to give animals human expressions. And when it comes to cartoons, it's always a good idea to exaggerate as much as possible for maximum silly effect!

Bear

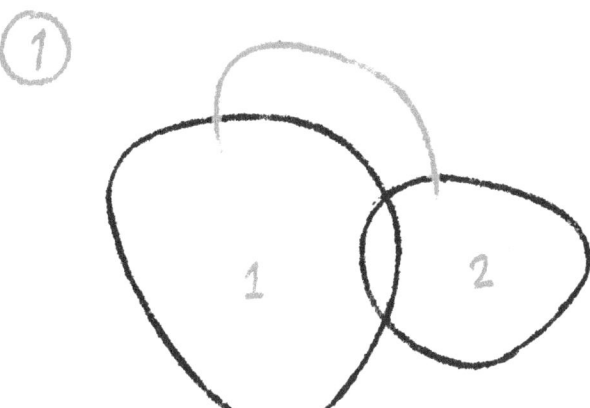

Shape 1 will be a big open mouth. Shape 2 will be the body. The shapes are connected by a line that will form the head.

Erase the overlapping lines and connect the body.

Draw the mouth, eyes, nose and ears. Then erase any extra lines.

Add the extra details on the mouth, draw a tail, then draw the legs.

Add the arms and the belly circle.

Finish by cleaning up any unwanted lines and finish shading in your bear.

TIPS & TRICKS

Drawing the animal close to the horizon line makes it look far away. The further away from the line that animal is, the bigger it looks!

HORIZON LINE

BACKGROUND (FAR AWAY)

MIDDLE GROUND

FOREGROUND

LEVEL UP!

Silly Clothing

Practice using the panda template to dress it with silly clothing items.

Use the first two pandas as reference.

Don't forget to draw a silly expression!

Learn how to draw these silly animals.

CHIRP & SOAR

Toucan

We're going to start by imagining 2 rectangles to draw the body and the toucan's beak.

Set up two rectangles to be used as guidelines for our toucan.

Split the right rectangle in half.

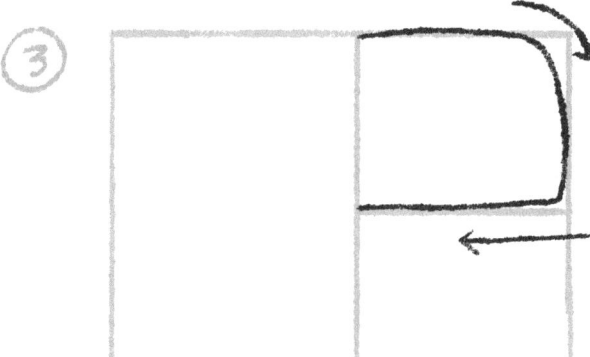

Now we can start by drawing the bill using the guidelines we set up.

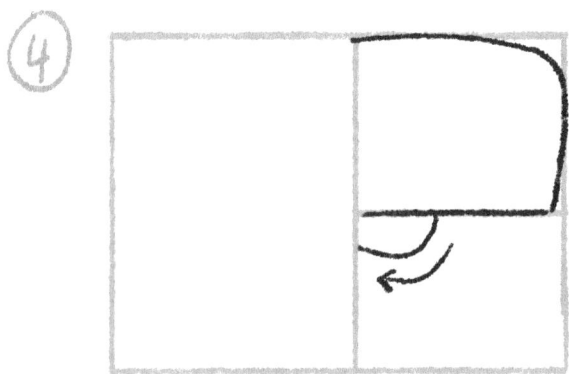

Draw the bottom for the mouth.

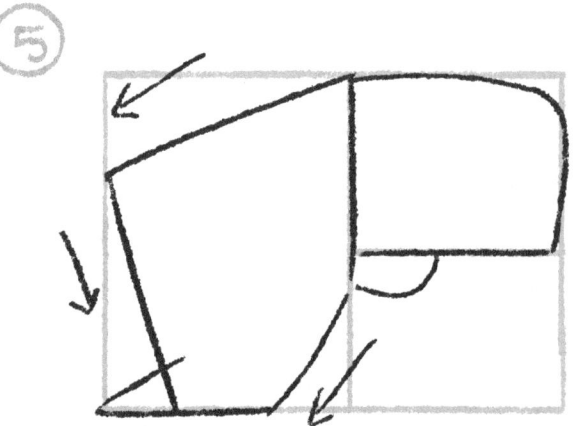

Next, start by drawing the basic shape of the body by using straight lines.

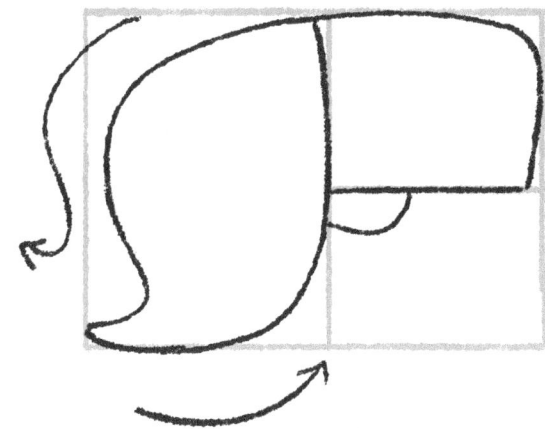

Reshape the straight lines to be more curved.

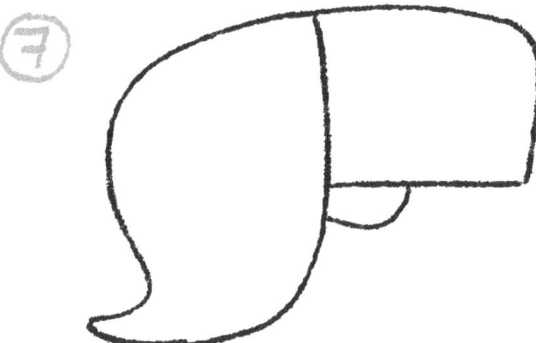

If you drew the guidelines, remove them now.

Now add the details, like the eyes, wings and legs.

Now you have a Toucan!

Practice

LEVEL UP!

Practice
How is your Toucan feeling in its cage?

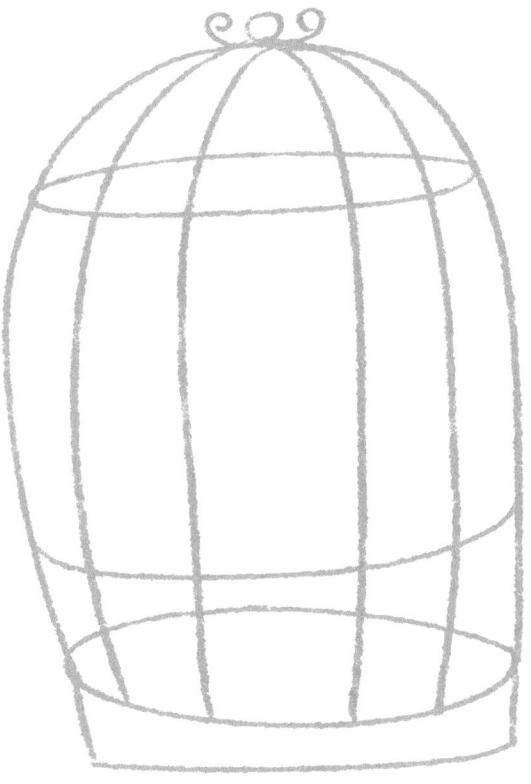
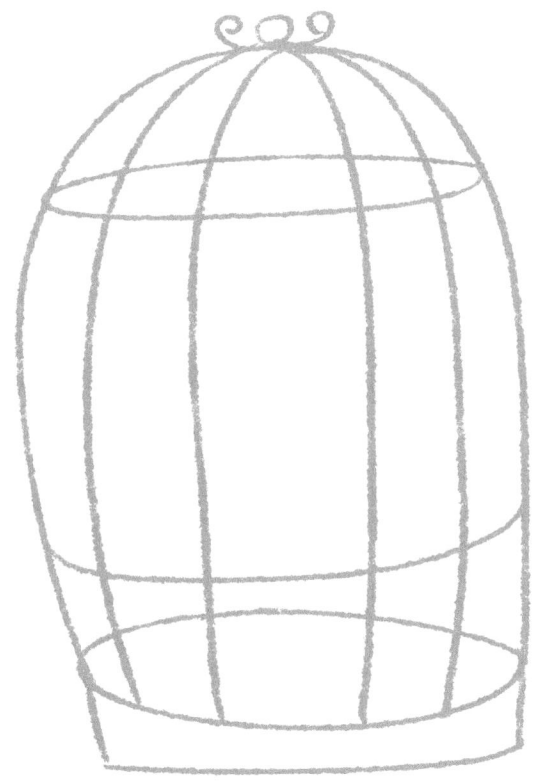
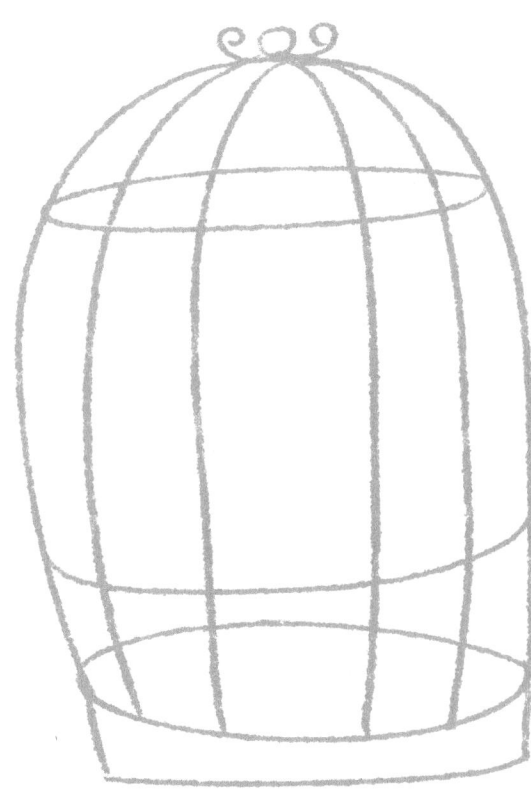

DID YOU KNOW?

Toucans serve an important ecological role as they disperse the seeds of the fruit they consume.

Their bills can be solid black, blue, brown, green, red, white, yellow, or colored patterns.

What is the toucan saying?

NOW WITH TWICE AS MANY WORMS!

Penguin

Penguins can be very fun and easy to draw. Let's start with 2 basic shapes.

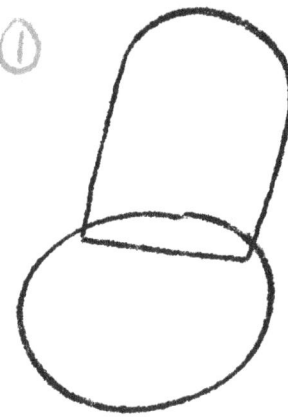

We can give it a round belly and a simple head.

Add the feet.

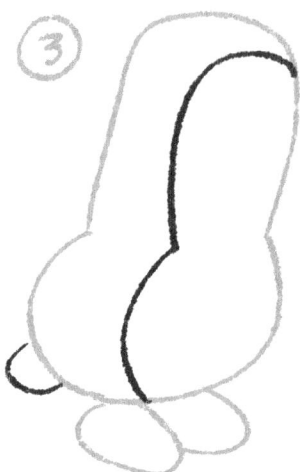

Draw the body line and tail.

Draw the beak, the wings and the googly eyes.

That's a silly penguin!

Practice

How many different kinds of silly penguins can you draw?

Flamingo

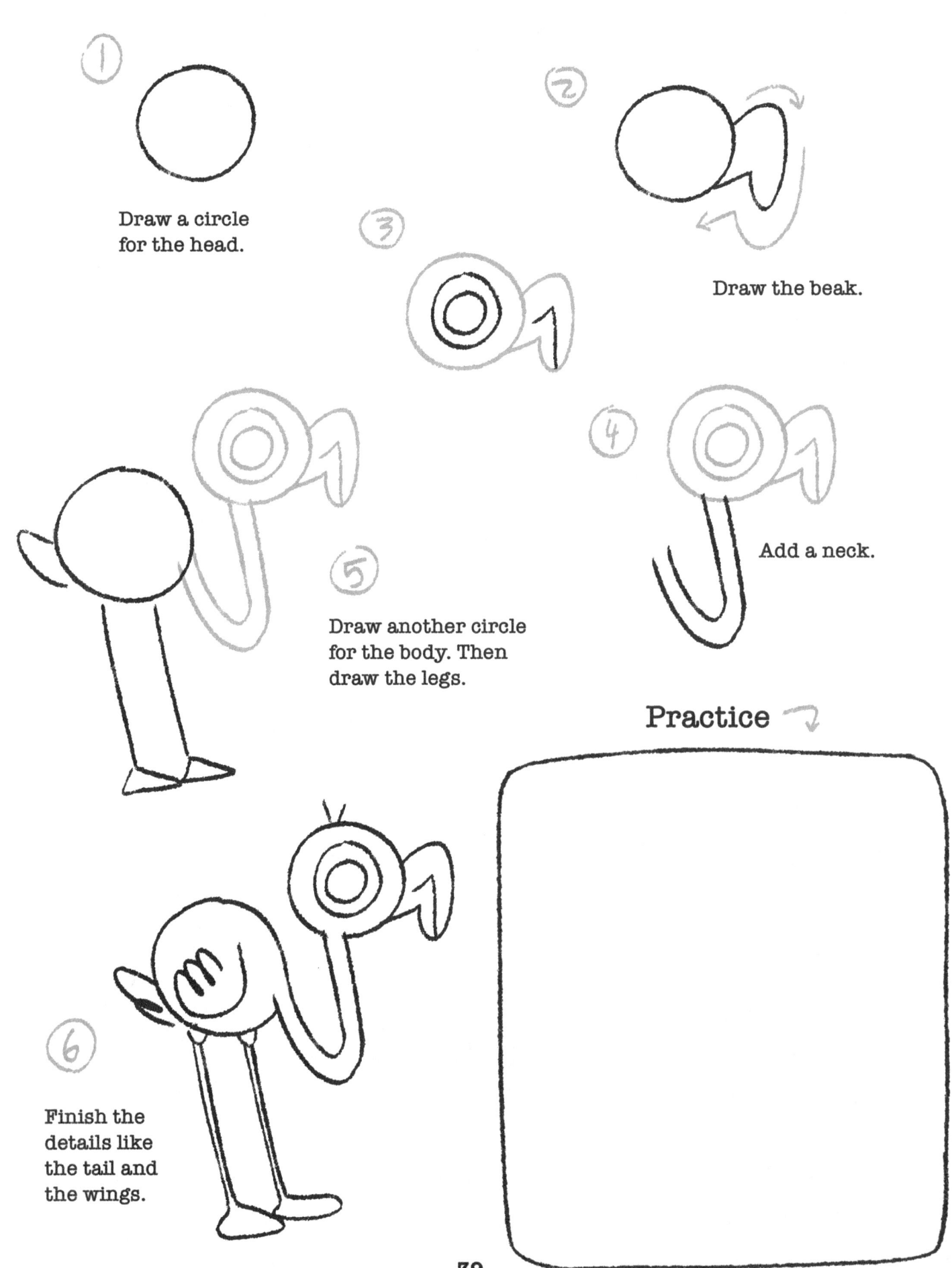

1. Draw a circle for the head.
2. Draw the beak.
3.
4. Add a neck.
5. Draw another circle for the body. Then draw the legs.
6. Finish the details like the tail and the wings.

Practice

LEVEL UP!

Give the flamingo a fun neck as shown in the example!

Example

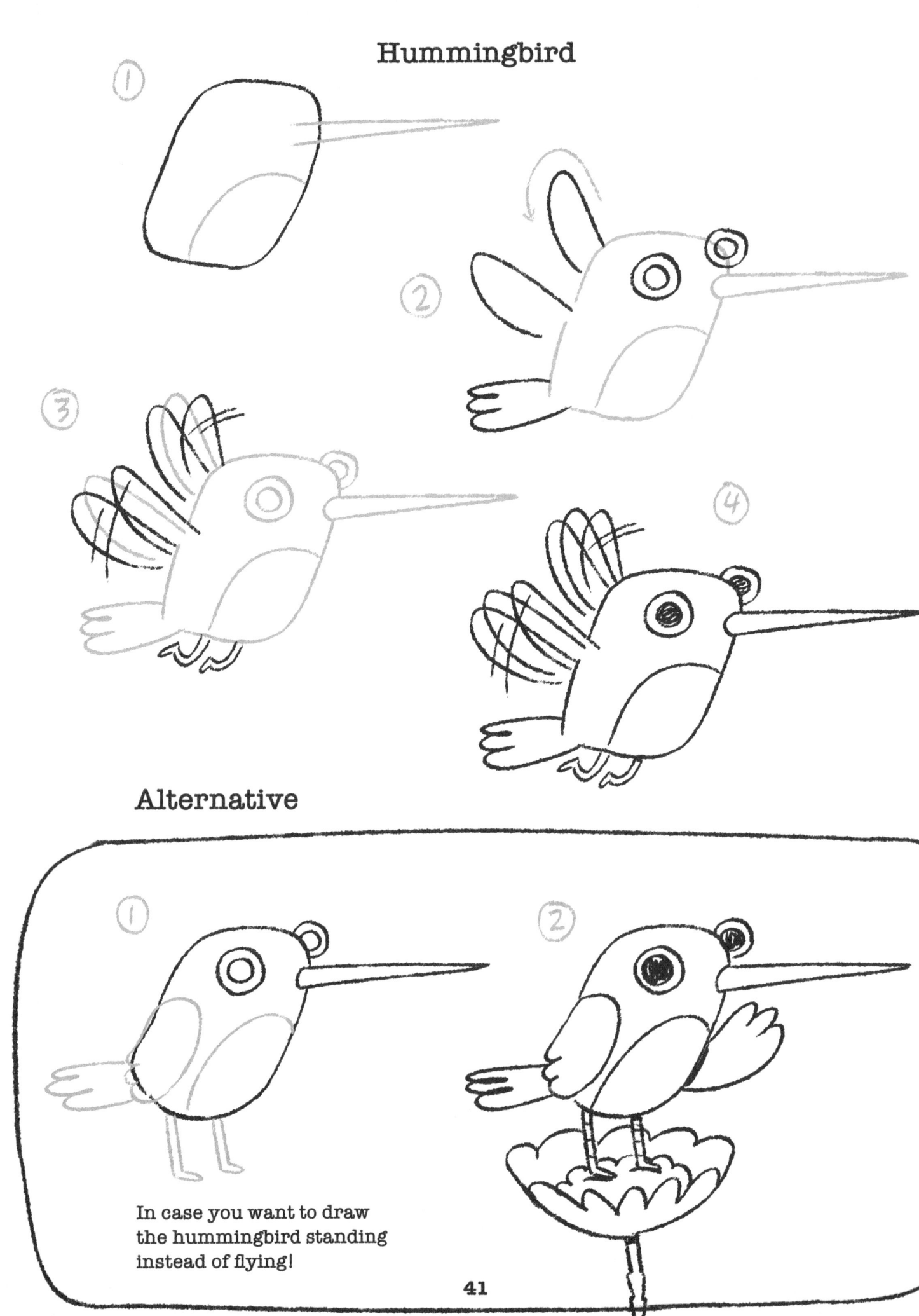

Crow

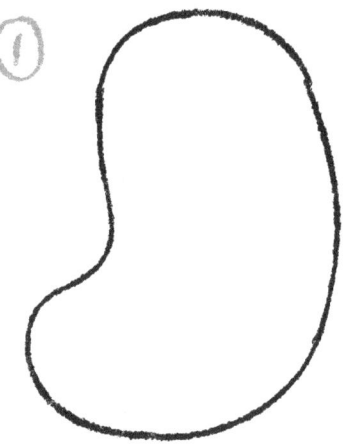

Draw a bean shape for the body.

Add a long beak, a tail, and the wings.

Draw the legs.

DID YOU KNOW?

Crows and ravens are some of the smartest animals in the world. They are considered to be as intelligent as chimpanzees.

The main differences between ravens and crows are their size and weight. Ravens are heavier and longer than crows.

Practice

Draw some crows around the scarecrow! Is the scarecrow working? Are your crows scared?

Rooster

The main difference between a rooster and a chicken is that the rooster stands straighter and has a bigger tail and crest.

Chicken

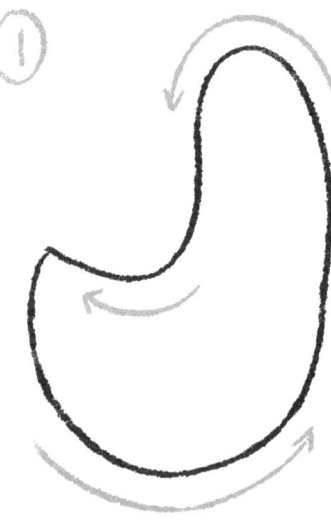

The chicken will have a smaller crest and a smaller tail.

FLAT CIRCLES

LEVEL UP!

When practicing drawing chickens or roosters, try exploring different body shapes and sizes.

Who came first the chicken or the egg?

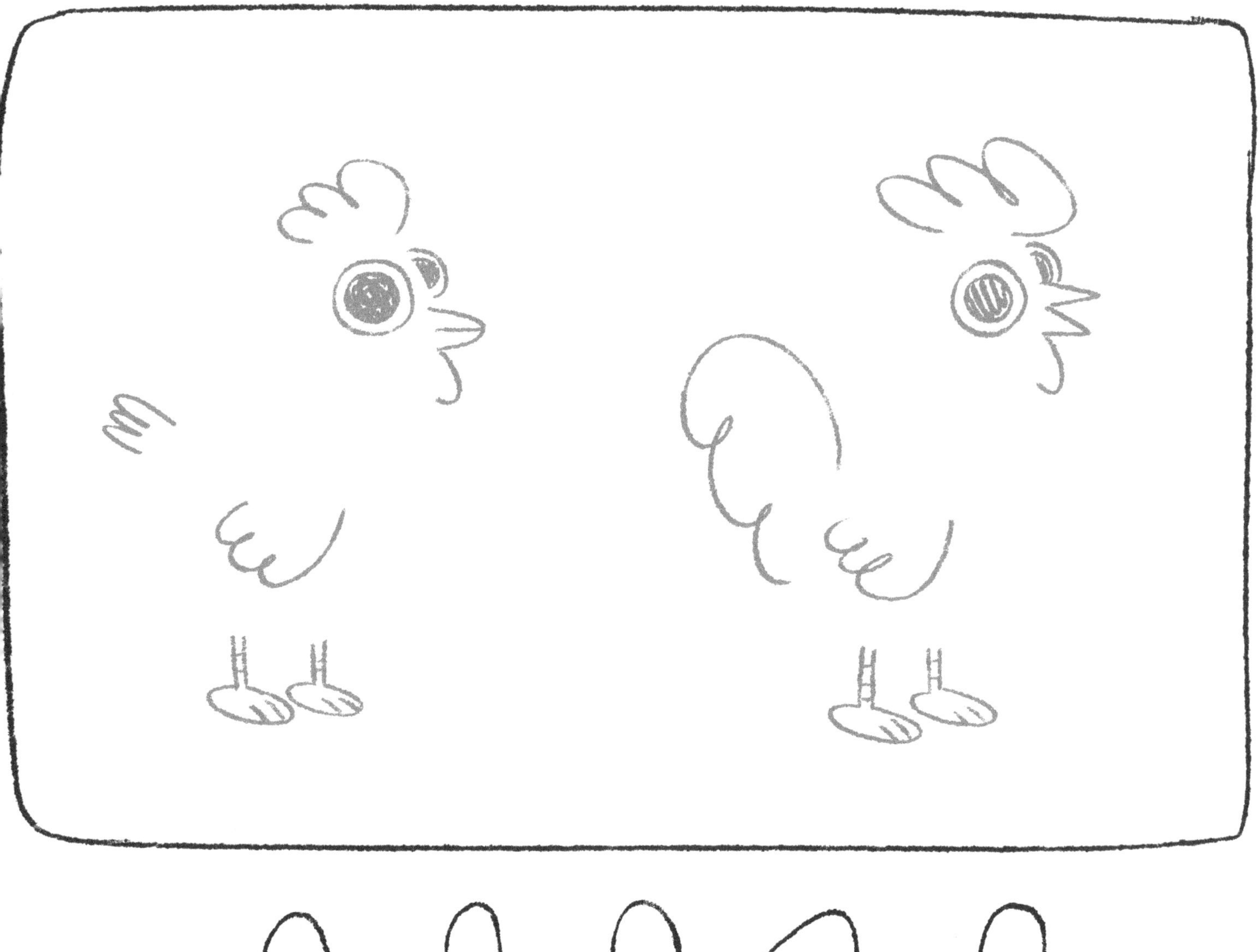

BODY SHAPE EXAMPLES

Duck

Start with simple shapes that contrast.

Draw big eyes and the bill.

Add a wing and a silly tail.

You can always round off the feet.

Maybe draw the other wing waving hello!

DID YOU KNOW?

Ducks eat rocks.

They store the rocks in their gizzards and use the rough textures to help with breaking down the food.

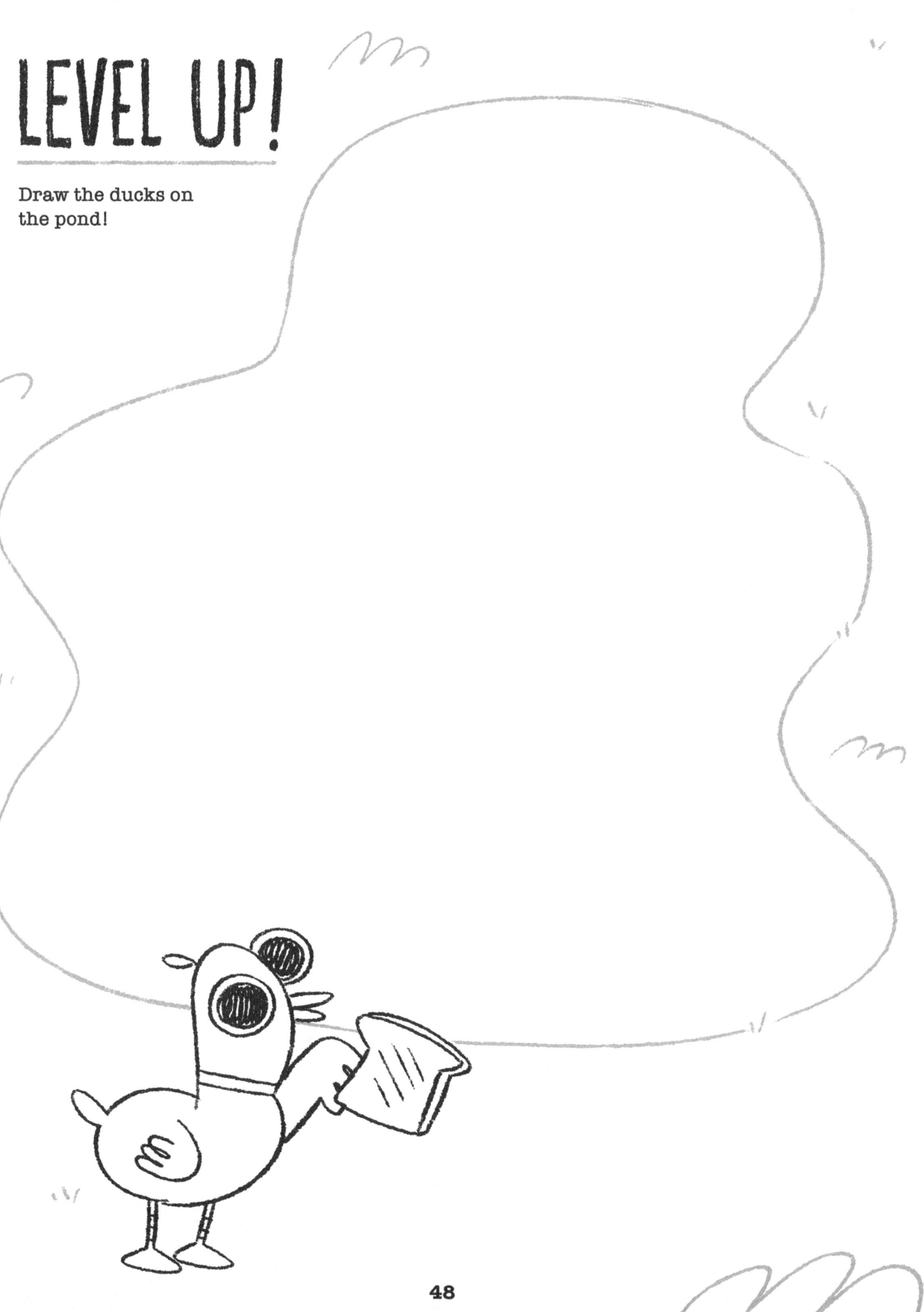

Parrot

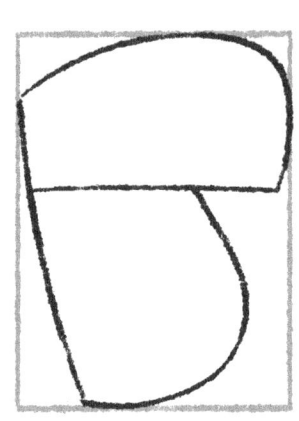

Use a guide to set up the body to beak proportions.

Once you shaped the body, erase the extra lines.

Draw a vertical line to separate the beak. Then add the tail.

Shape the mouth.

Add the wings.

Add the feet.

Finish your parrot with some extra fun details.

LEVEL UP!

Make your parrot fly.

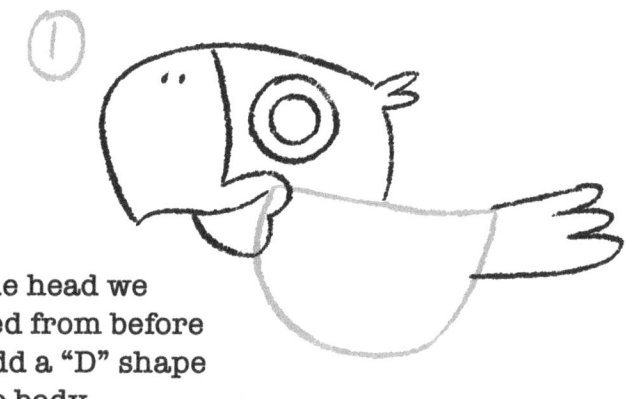

Use the head we learned from before and add a "D" shape for the body

Add the wing going up or down to show movement.

You can make it fly by drawing them in a flip book!

Practice

Owl

Start with a rectangle with a sharp corner and a soft one.

Add the eyes.

Give it a fun brow and set the wings.

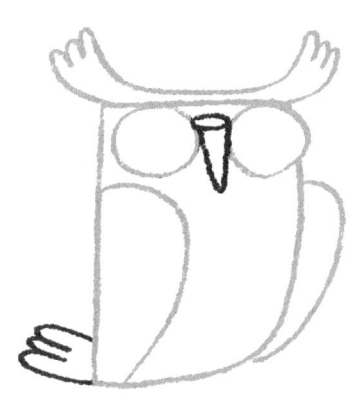

Draw the beak in the middle of the eyes and add the tail.

Add the legs.

Finish by giving it detail.

Practice

Owl

DID YOU KNOW?

There are over 250 type of owls in the world.

BUZZ & CRAWL

Learn how to draw these silly characters.

FLY

BUTTERFLY

SPIDER

CRICKET

BEE

ANT

BEETLE

LADYBUG

MOSQUITO

SNAIL
(NOT AN ACTUAL BUG)

Cricket

Draw a half circle for the head. Make it as big or as small as you want.

Add the body as a rounded rectangle.

Add the eyes at the ends of the head.

Draw the mouth. This bug is happy!

Draw horizontal lines on the body for that bug look.

Draw the wings to the sides.

Draw the antennas.

Add the arms and legs.

Add some shading and you're done!

Practice ↷

LEVEL UP!

When drawing a character and you want to give it a personality or an emotion, it is important to understand all the many emotions and how to put them on paper. Here are some examples that can help you give your character life.

Practice here

TIPS & TRICKS

The silhouette of your character should be easy to recognize.

Use shapes to help make drawing difficult characters simple!

You can see how complex characters are comprised of basic shapes.

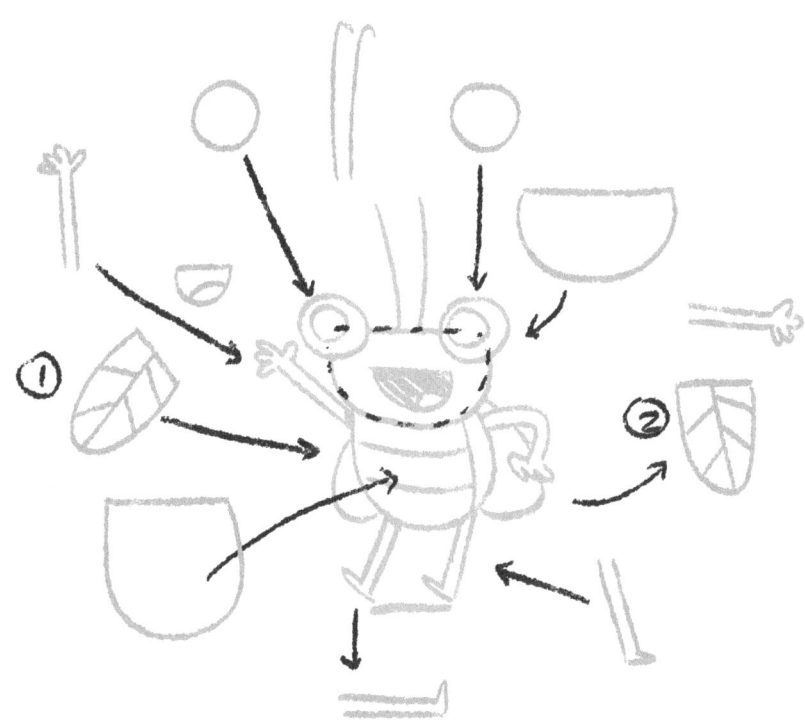

DID YOU KNOW?

Rubbing Wings Makes Music. Crickets sing an impressive variety of songs, each with its own purpose. A male's calling song invites receptive females to come closer. He then serenades the female with his courtship song.

LEVEL UP!

Understanding the head means you can draw the face from different angles. Follow these tips to help you draw from different angles.

①

Stack three circles to form the body.

Changing how you stack the circles will change the ant's pose!

②

Decide where your ant is looking. Use a cross to help guide where you place the eyes.

③

For a fun look, give big pincers to the ant.

④

Add the legs and antennas.

⑤

Add extra arms. Ants have 6 legs!

⑥

Once you finish, try giving the character something to do.

Ladybug

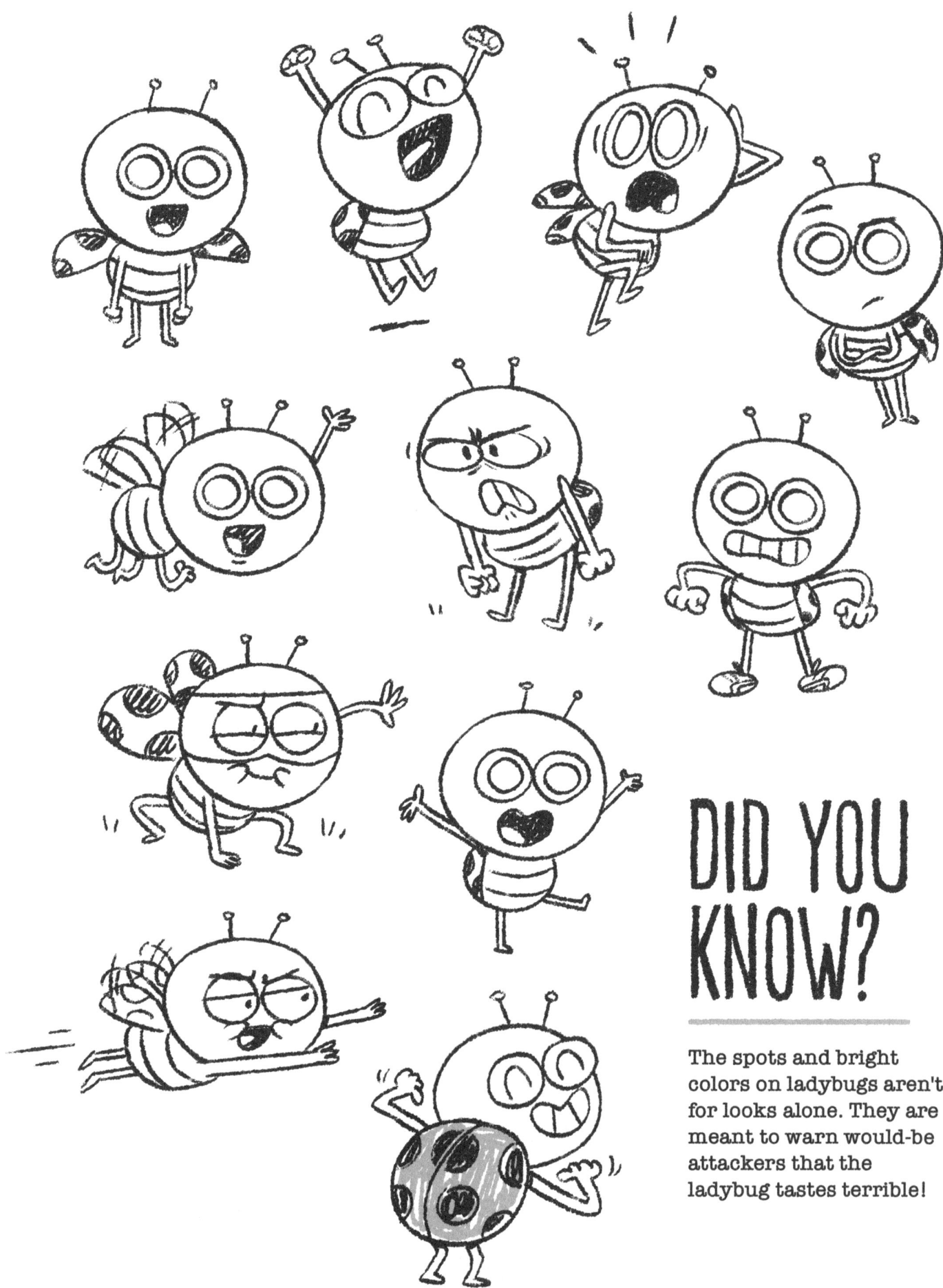

DID YOU KNOW?

The spots and bright colors on ladybugs aren't for looks alone. They are meant to warn would-be attackers that the ladybug tastes terrible!

TIPS & TRICKS

Try playing with proportions. Use different sized shapes to create fun characters!

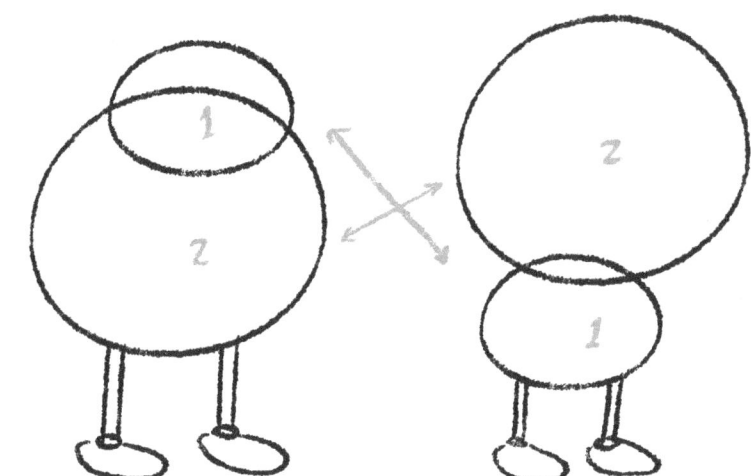

Practice

Fly

Draw two big circles for the eyes.

Add a straw for the mouth.

Draw the body.

Add the arms and legs (they are hanging because he's flying).

Draw two wings from the back.

Finish adding all the extra details.

Practice

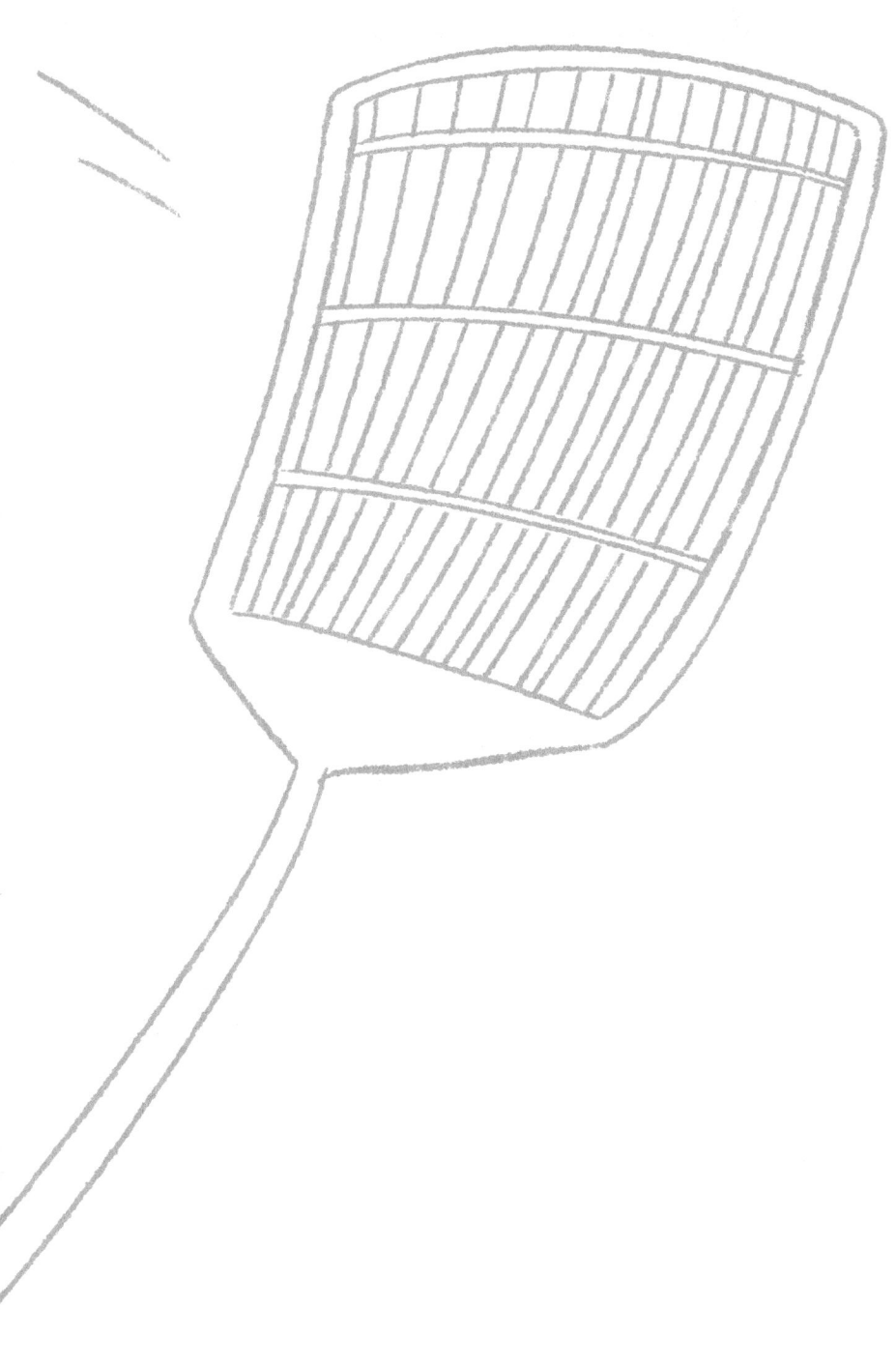

Draw a bunch of flies flying away from the swatter!

Spider

Start with 2 circles, a big one and a small one.

Draw the face and give it pincers for a mouth.

Spiders have 8 legs.

Finish drawing the legs and shade in for details!

Practice

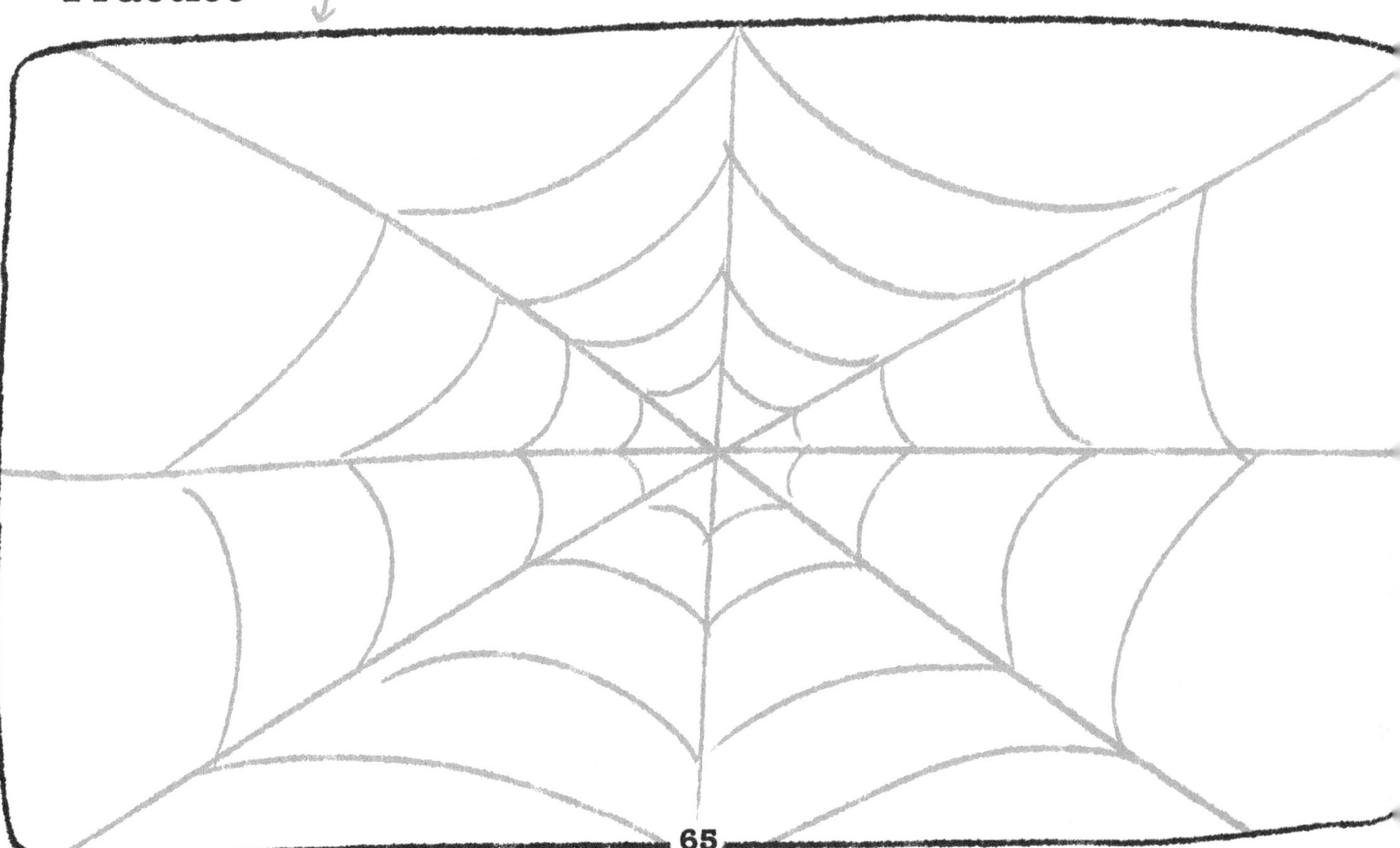

Spiders are arachnids, a class of arthropods that also includes scorpions, mites, and ticks.

There are over 46,700 species of arachnids! Arachnids differ from insects in that they have 8 instead of 6 legs, and have a body that is divided into 2 parts, instead of 3.

The majority of spiders have eight eyes and are extremely short-sighted. Spiders' legs are covered in microscopic hairs that help them hear and smell.

Spiders, unlike insects, do not have antennae.

DID YOU KNOW?

All spiders make silk.

Butterfly

Start with a circle for the head and a long, thin shape for the body.

Add the wings in the back.

Draw the face.

Add details for the wings.

Draw the arms and legs.

Finish by cleaning up the extra lines and details.

Practice

Draw some silly wing patterns. You can also color them!

Bee

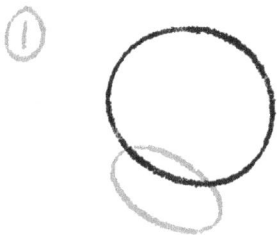

Draw 2 circles for the head and thorax.

Follow the lines to draw a more stylized abdomen.

Add the eyes and antennas.

Add the wings and the abdomen lines.

Add the arms, legs, and finishing details!

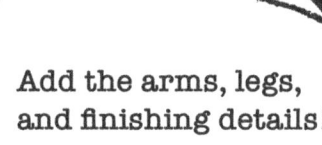

Practice

REALISTIC

CARTOON

SIMPLIFIED

Practice

DID YOU KNOW?

Snails are not bugs or insects, even though they share some of the same traits and behaviors.

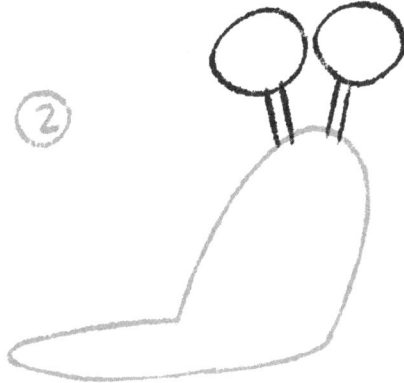

Snails are gastropods that can live on land or in water.

Gastropods are a group of invertebrates (animals that don't have spines) that are separated into two groups: slugs and snails.

SLUG   SNAIL

LEVEL UP!

Turn the slugs into snails.

← DRAW THEIR HOUSES

Here are some ideas for you to draw.

DID YOU KNOW?

The hercules beetle is a species of rhinoceros beetle, which contains over 1500 species that include unicorn beetles and horn beetles.

Only males have horns.

Add the two shapes for the head and the body. Then add the famous horns on top.

Draw a silly face, then add the body lines.

Finish by giving it arms and legs.

Practice

WHAT IS HE LIFTING?

Draw something big and heavy that the beetle is lifting!

HOP & SLITHER

Learn how to draw these silly characters.

Chameleon

To begin, you're going to connect these three shapes.

Once you overlay the shapes you can erase the middle (overlapping lines).

Or you can try drawing the outline on the first try.

Draw the mouth.

Draw the legs

Draw a circle as a guide for the tail, then draw your tail inside the circle.

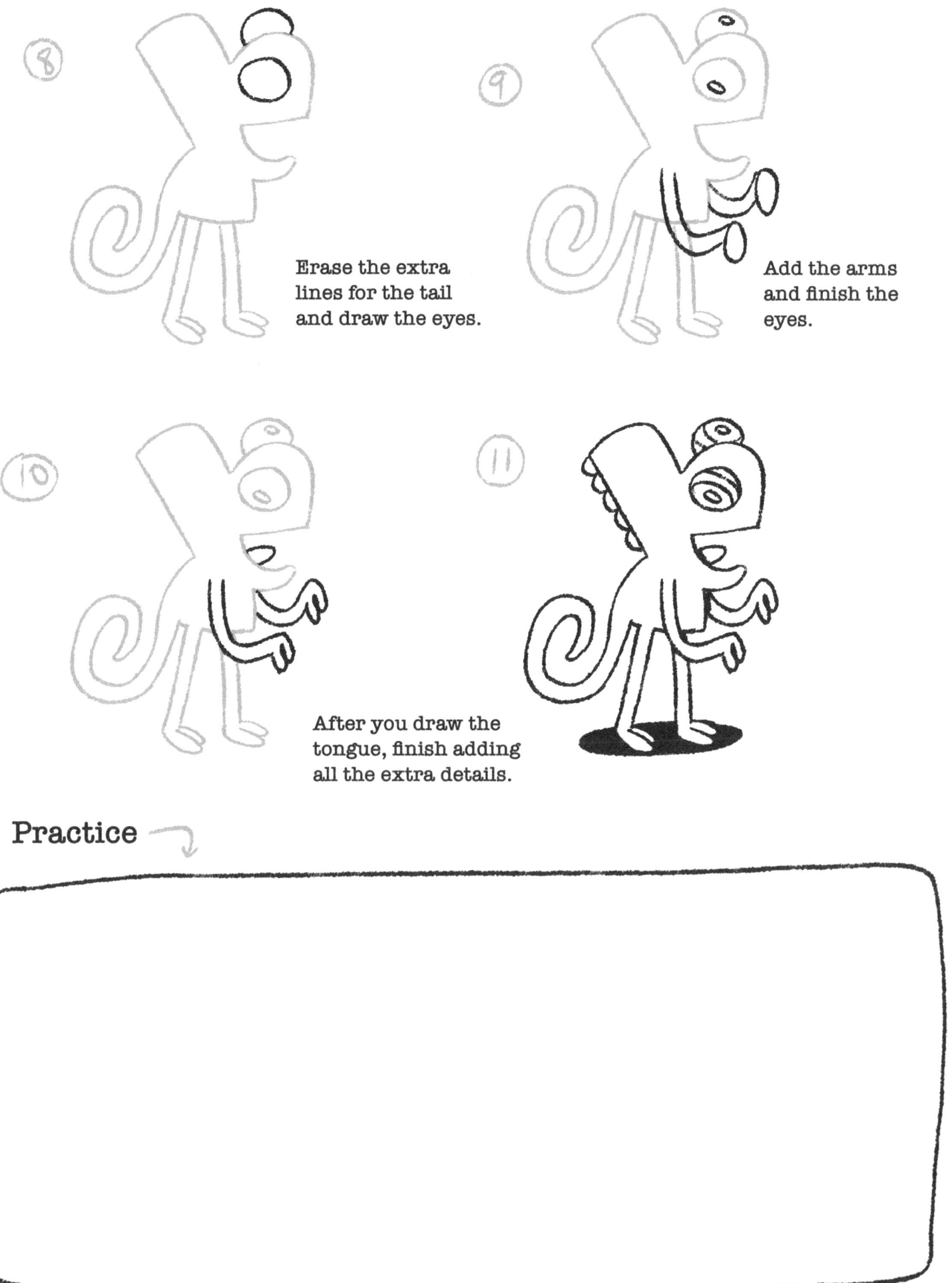

WHAT DID THE CHAMELEON CATCH?

Frog

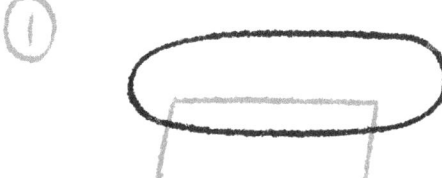

Draw a flat circle for the head and a rectangle for the body.

Erase the overlapping lines and then draw the mouth. Erase the extra lines so the mouth is open.

After drawing the mouth, draw the arms and legs.

Finish by drawing the details.

Practice

DID YOU KNOW?

Frogs are different from reptiles because they don't have scaly skin!

Alligator

Make an "L" shape as guide for the head.

After you draw the head make a rectangle as a guide for the body.

Draw the tail and legs.

Erase all the guidelines and add the finishing details.

Ground it by adding backgroung details.

Crocodile

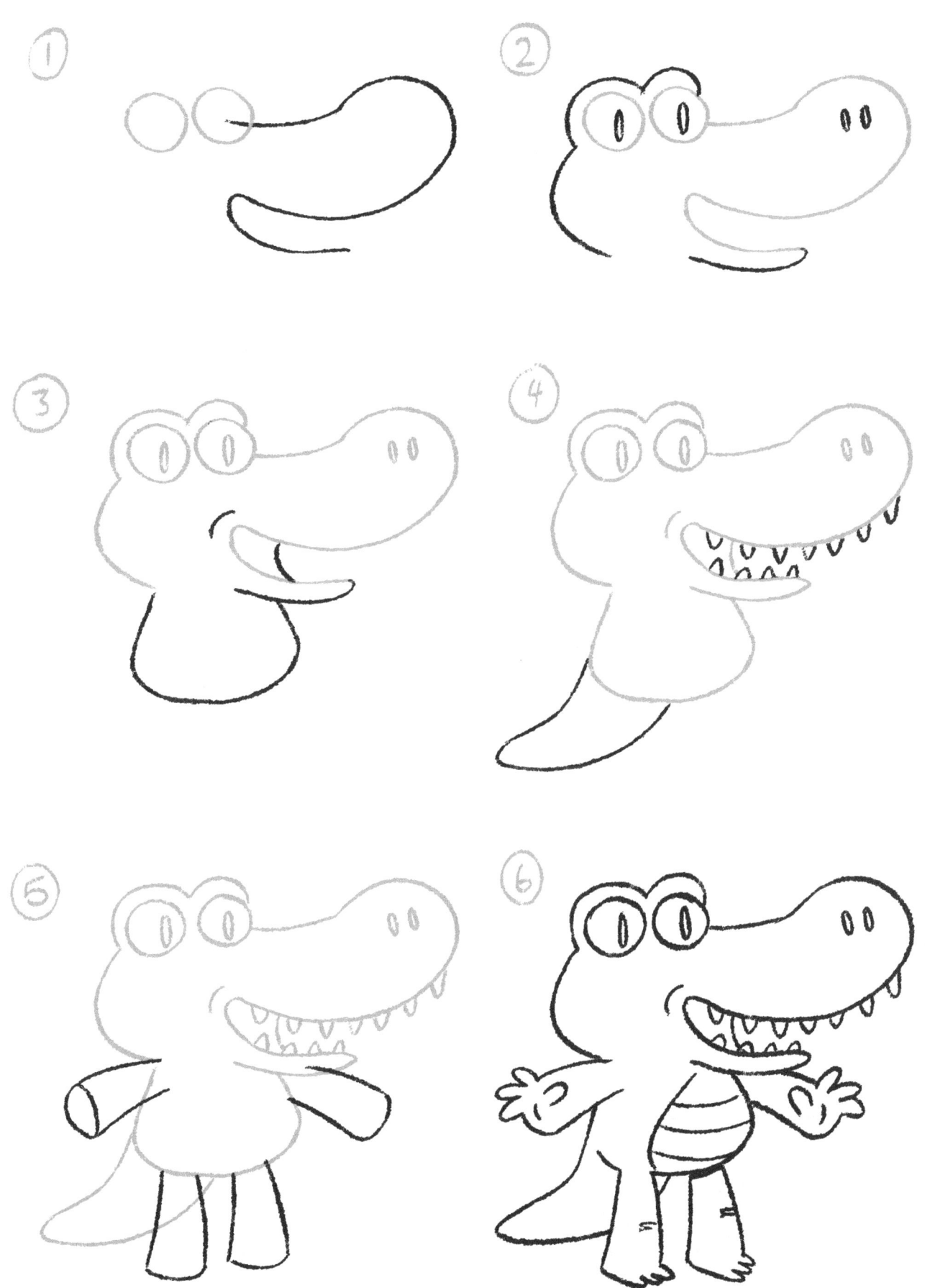

WHO IS THE CROCODILE SCARING?

Lizard

Draw an oval shape for the head.

Draw the eyes, then the body.

Draw a silly face and the tail.

Add the arms and legs.

Clean up the extra lines and finish the details.

Practice

Salamander

Draw a circle for the head.

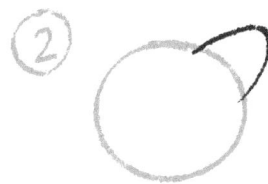
Add a mountain shape for the mouth.

Add the body and erase the extra lines.

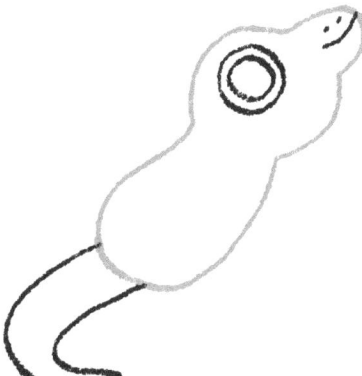
Draw a silly face then add the tail.

Add the arms and legs.

Clean up the extra lines and finish the details.

Practice

Gecko

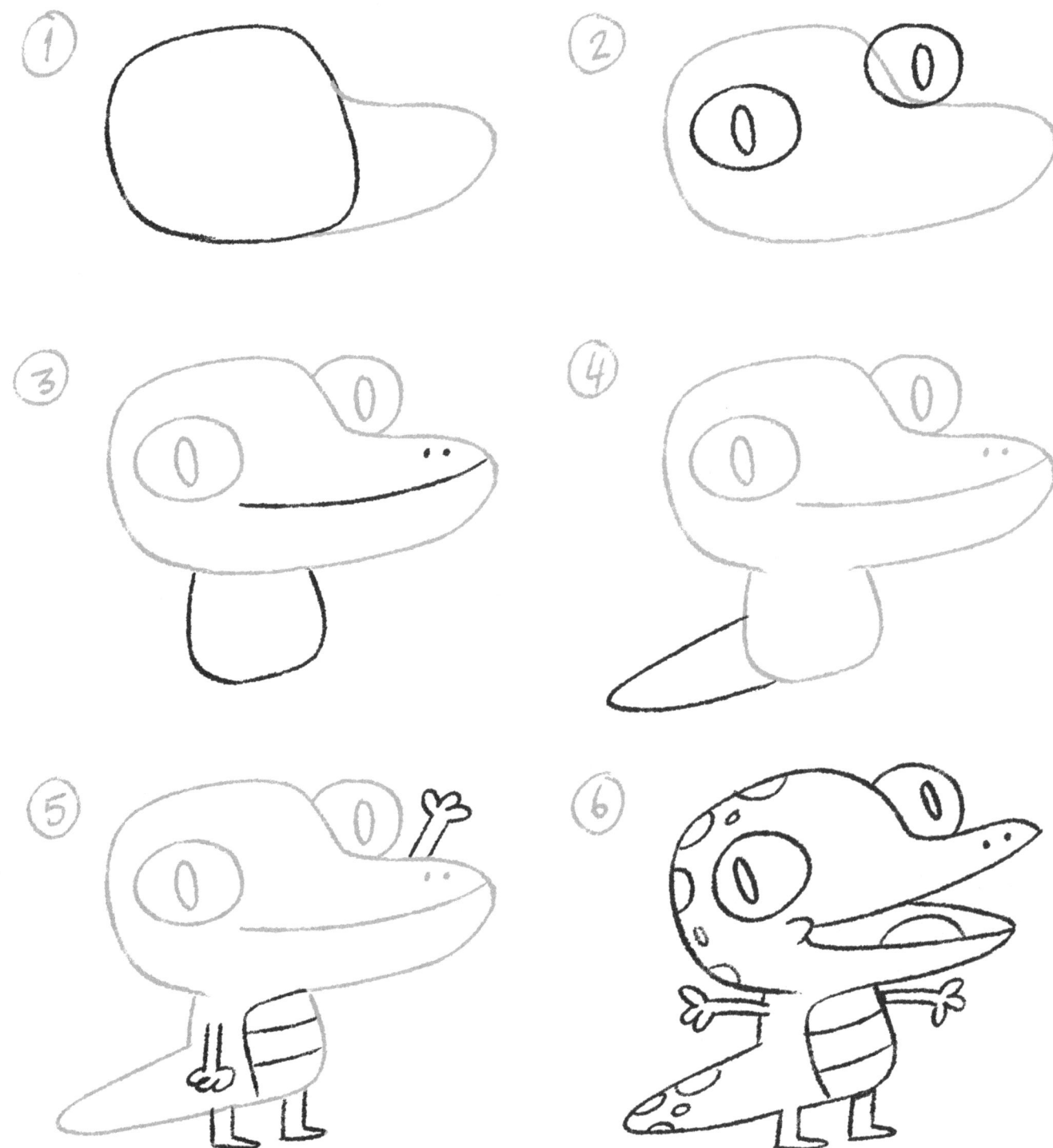

DID YOU KNOW?

- Geckos' amazing toes help them stick to any surface except Teflon.
- Most geckos can detach their tails and regrow them.
- Geckos' eyes are 350 times more sensitive to light than human eyes.
- Some species of geckos have no legs and look more like snakes.

LEVEL UP!

Give your gecko a silly personality.

Practice

88

DID YOU KNOW?

Frogs

Frogs are amphibians, without the tails! They are cold-blooded and can live on both land and in water.

Frogs have a visual field of almost 360° so they can look completely around themselves all the time!

Draw a gummy drop.

Draw two circles for eyes.

Set the foundation for the legs.

Think of the number 3 while adding the toes.

Add the finishing touches to show how your frog is feeling today!

Toad

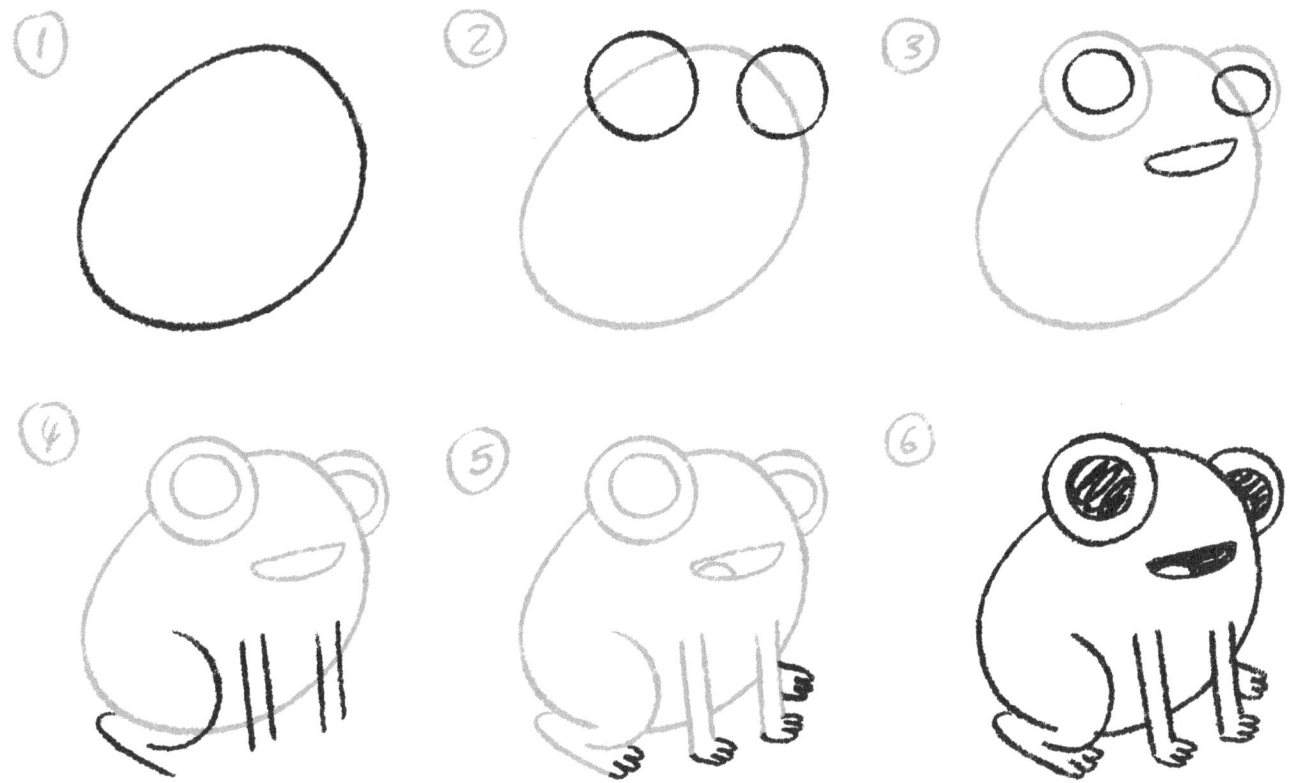

Practice

Snake

Use a square as a guide to draw the head.

Draw silly eyes, nostrils, fangs, and a tongue!

Add an "S" shape for the body and finish the final details.

Practice

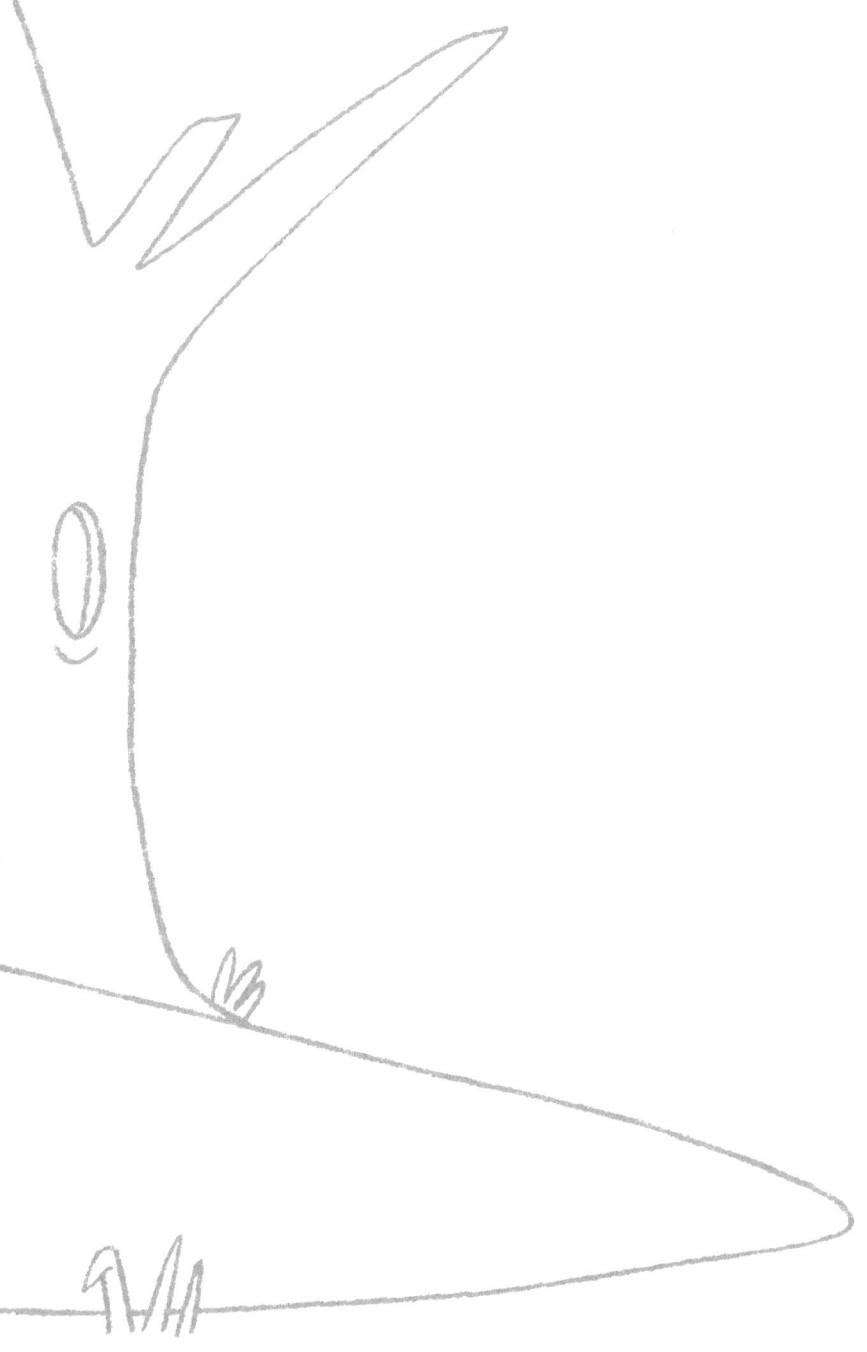

Draw what you've learned!

SPLASH & SWIM

Learn how to draw these silly characters.

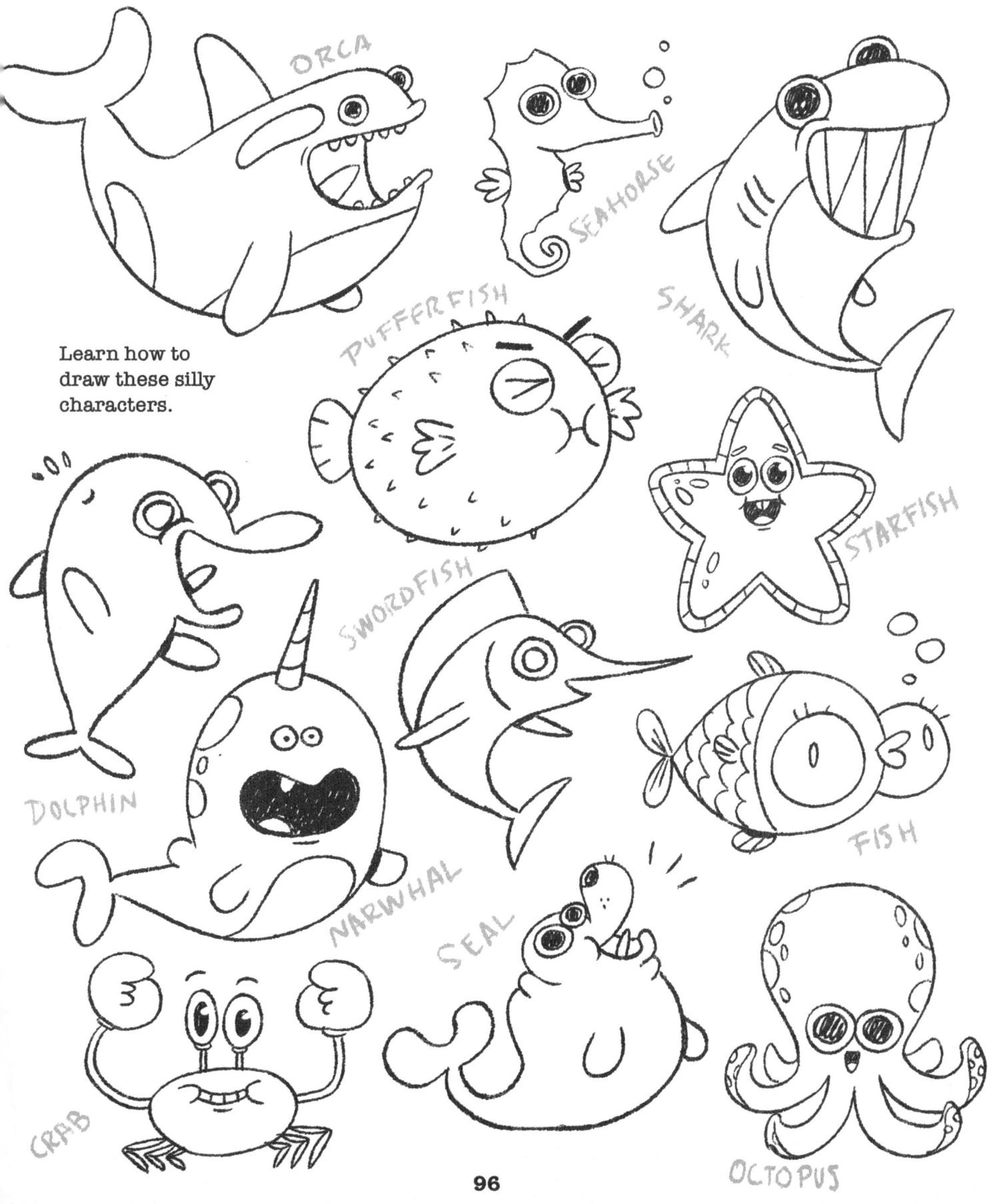

Dolphin

Draw a flat mountain.

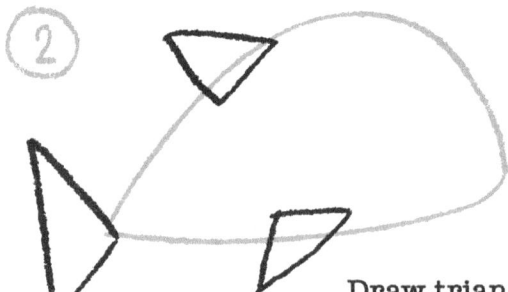

Draw triangles for the flippers.

Round the flippers then add the mouth and eyes.

Practice

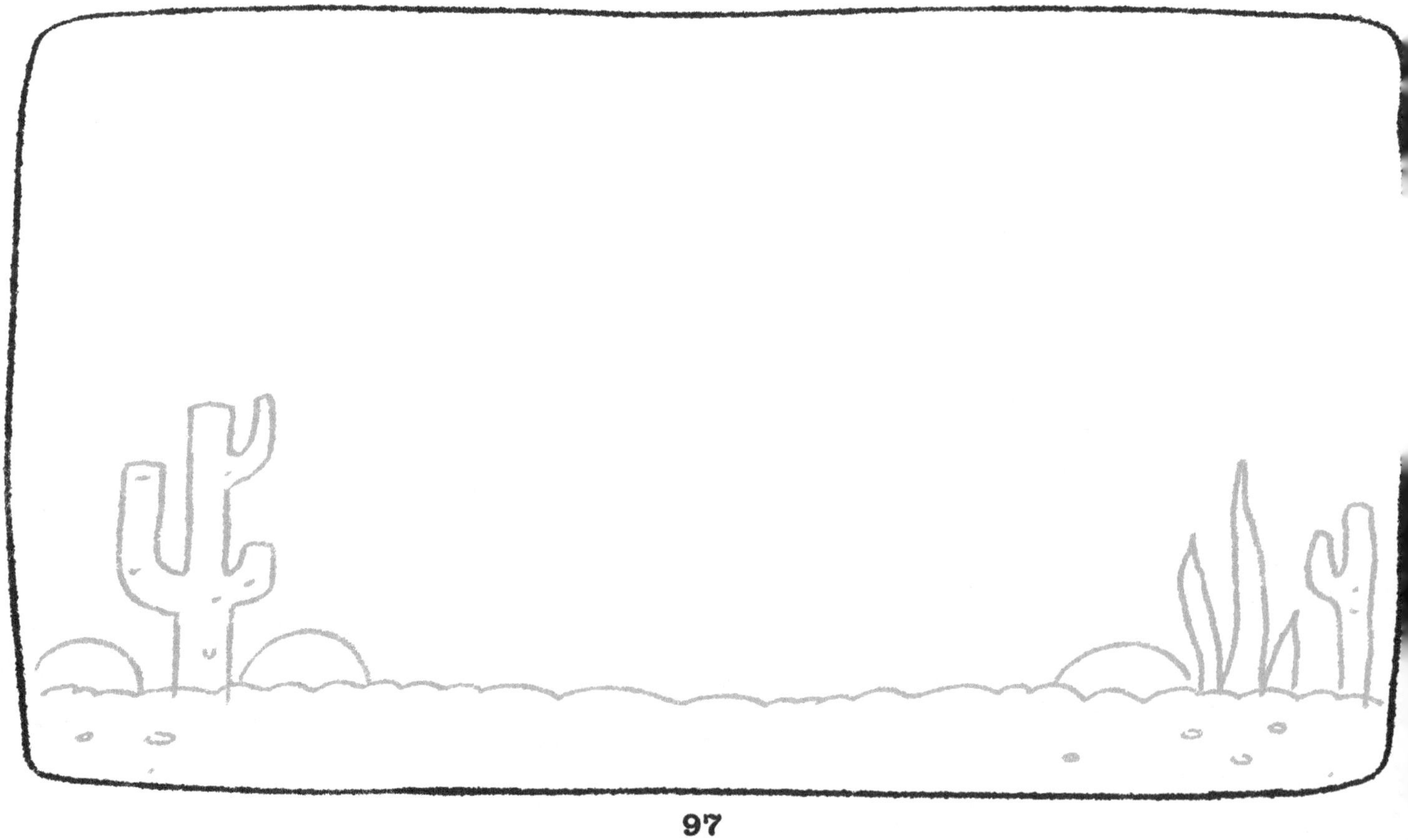

LEVEL UP!

Draw a dolphin using a different shape! Draw an upside down teardrop and then add the flippers and a silly face.

Practice

Crab

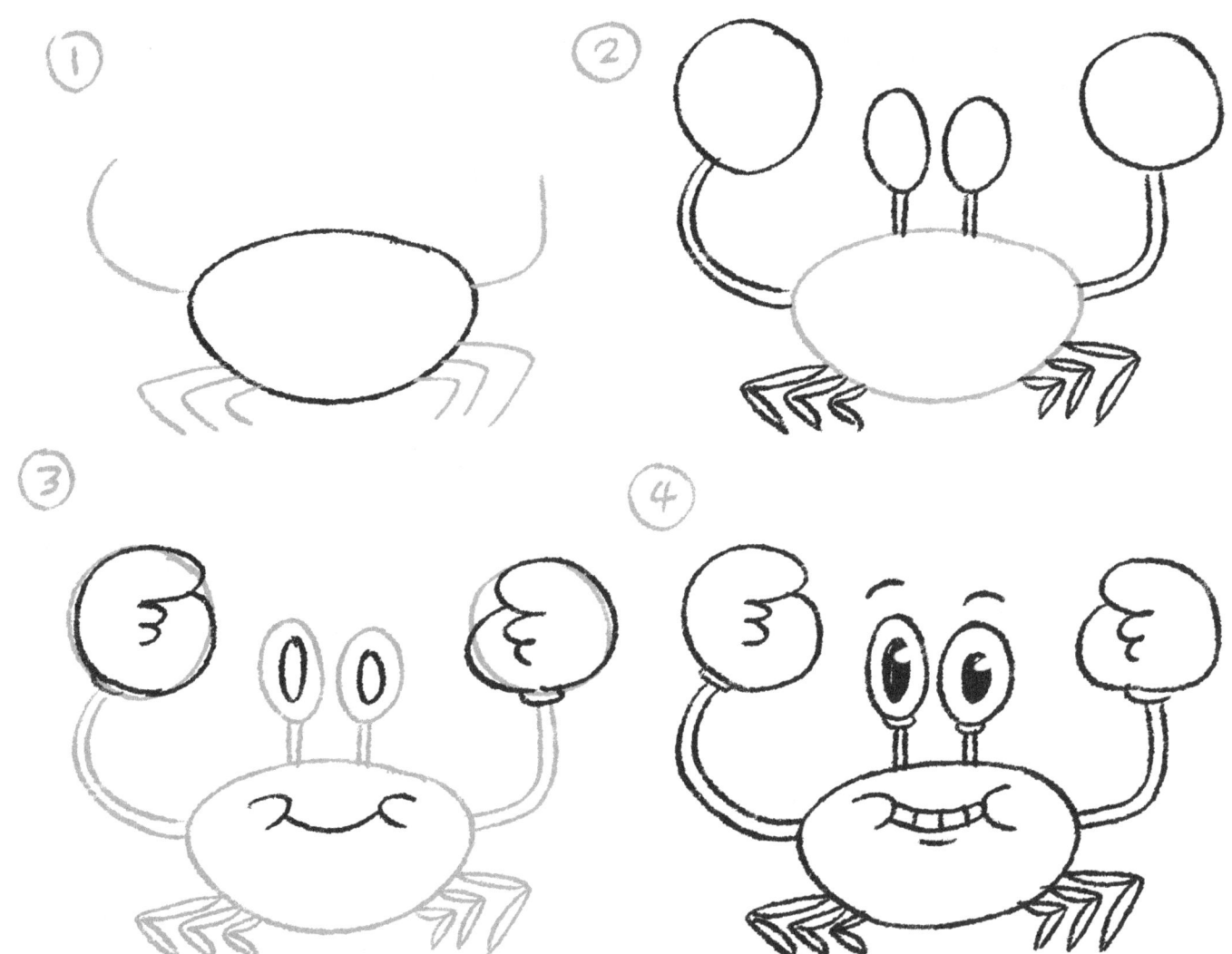

Practice

WHO LIVES ON THE SANDCASTLE?

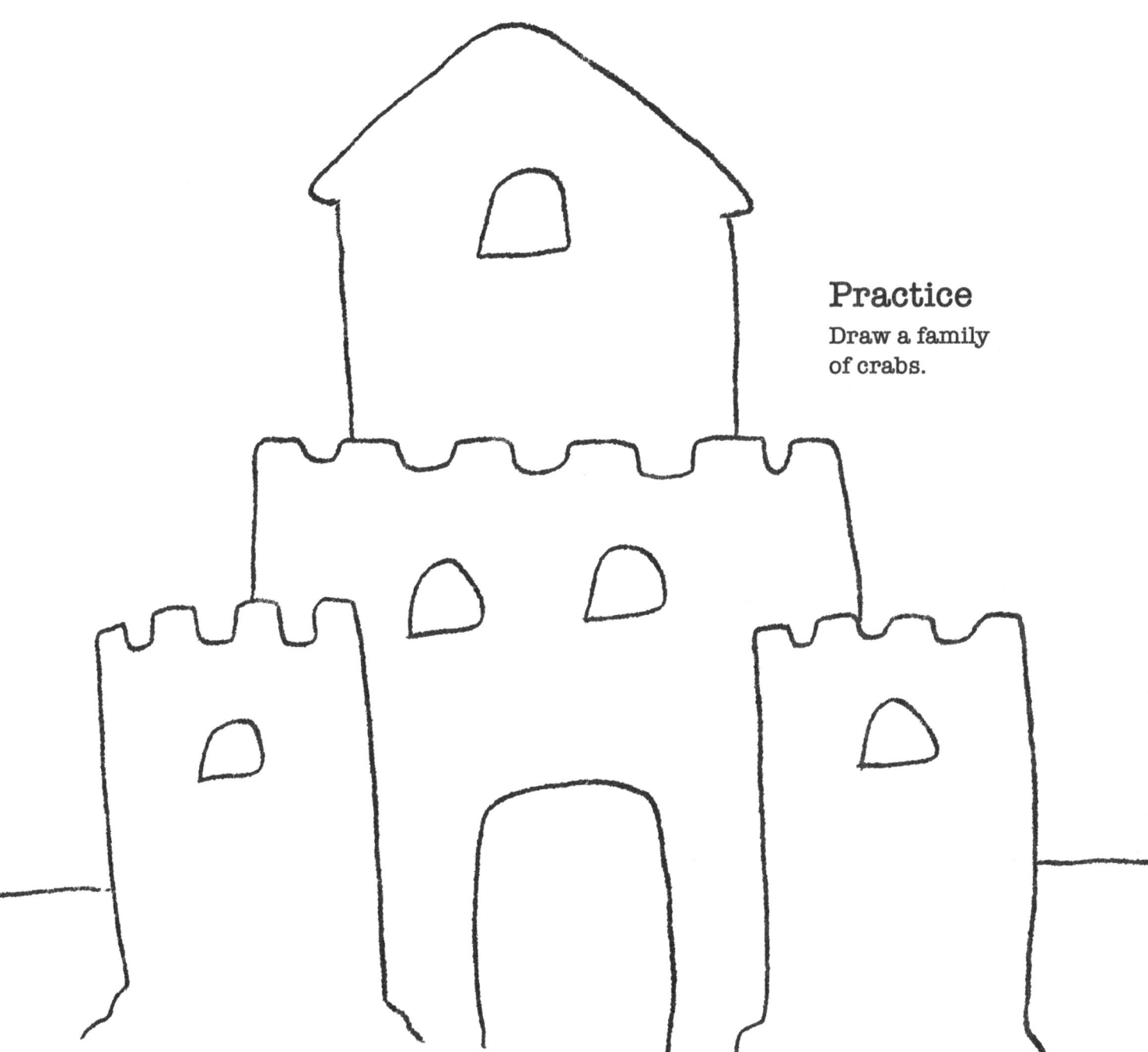

Practice
Draw a family of crabs.

Seahorse

Use a circle as a guide for the head and two lines for the snout.

Draw the head and snout. Use a guide for the body in the shape of the letter "D."

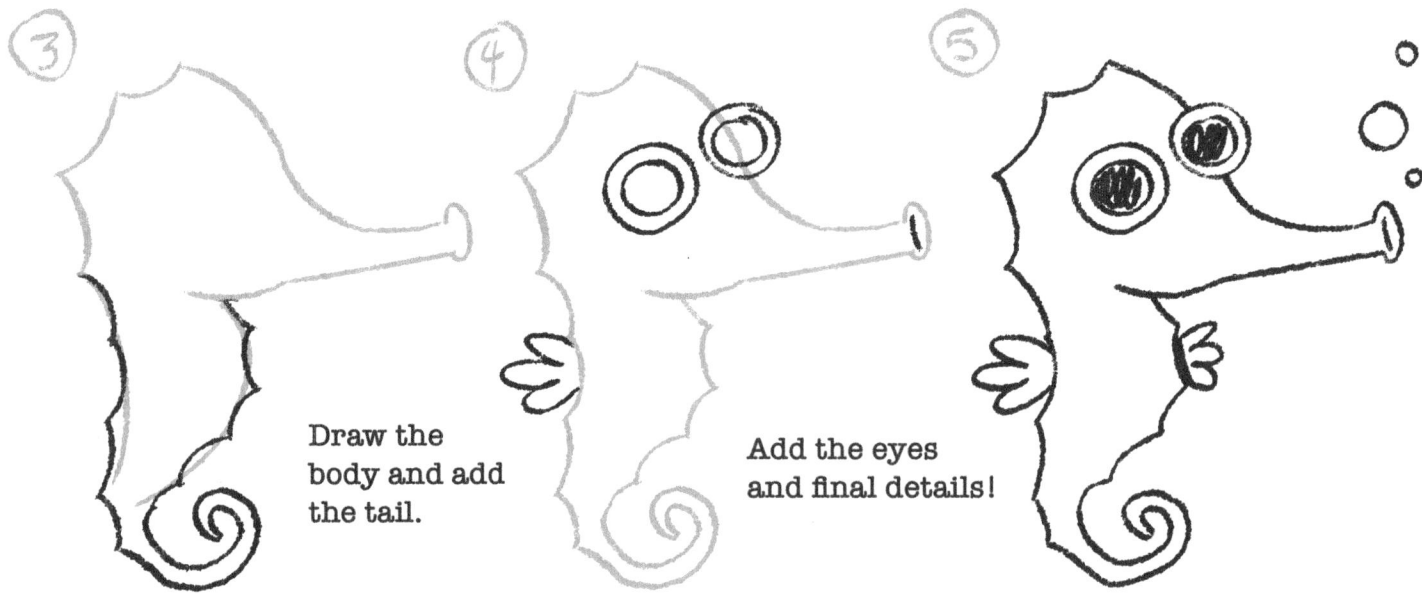

Draw the body and add the tail.

Add the eyes and final details!

Practice

Pufferfish

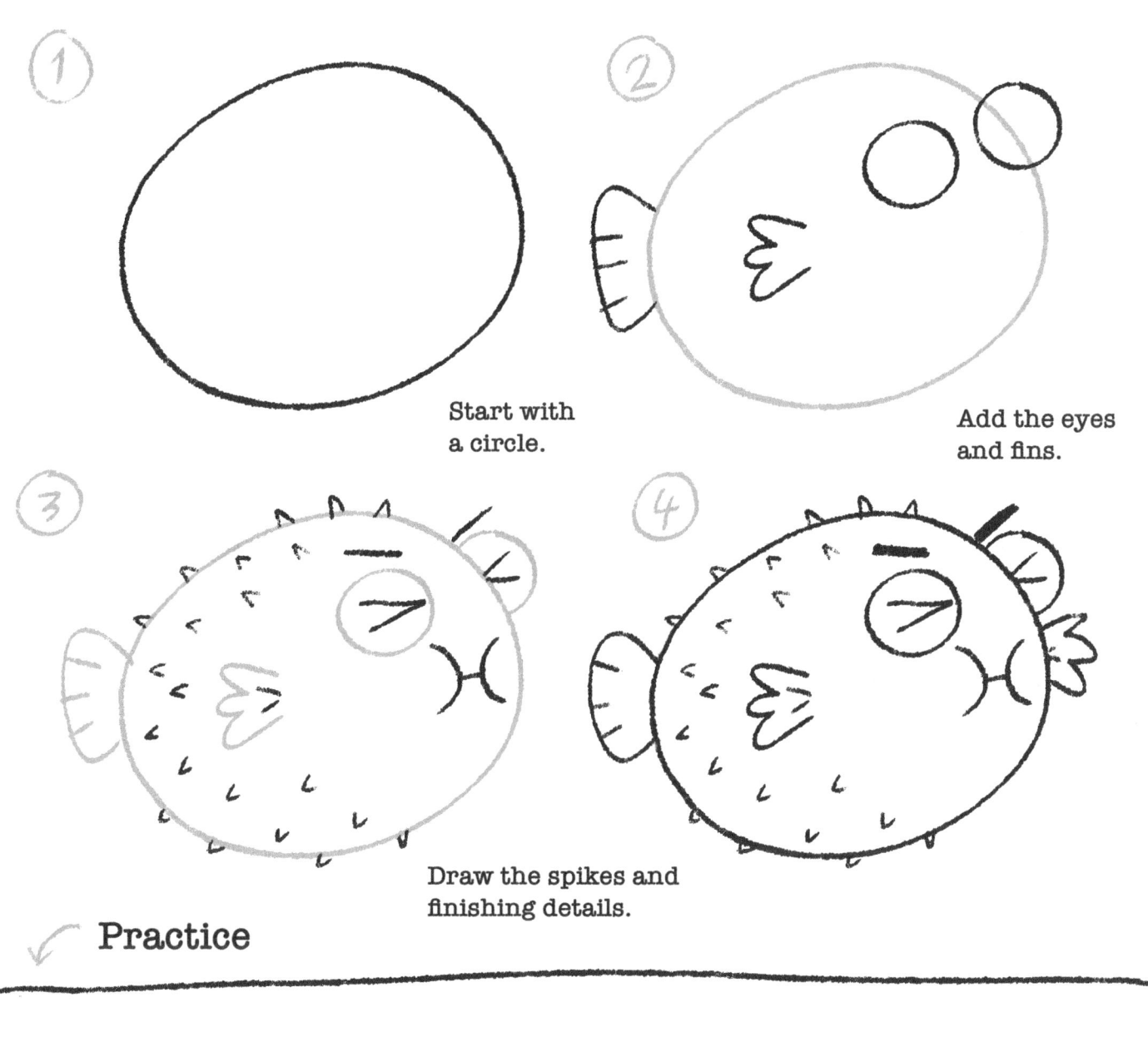

Start with a circle.

Add the eyes and fins.

Draw the spikes and finishing details.

Practice

Seal

Start wih a circle and then shape the snout.

Give it a smile and then shape the body following the arrows.

Once you draw the body, add the flippers and eyes.

Finish by erasing the extra lines and shading in the finishing details.

Practice

DID YOU KNOW?

- The closest living relatives to seals on land are believed to be dogs and bears.
- Seals can dive to great depths underwater and stay there for up to two hours.
- Seals use clicking or trilling noises to communicate.

Octopus

Practice

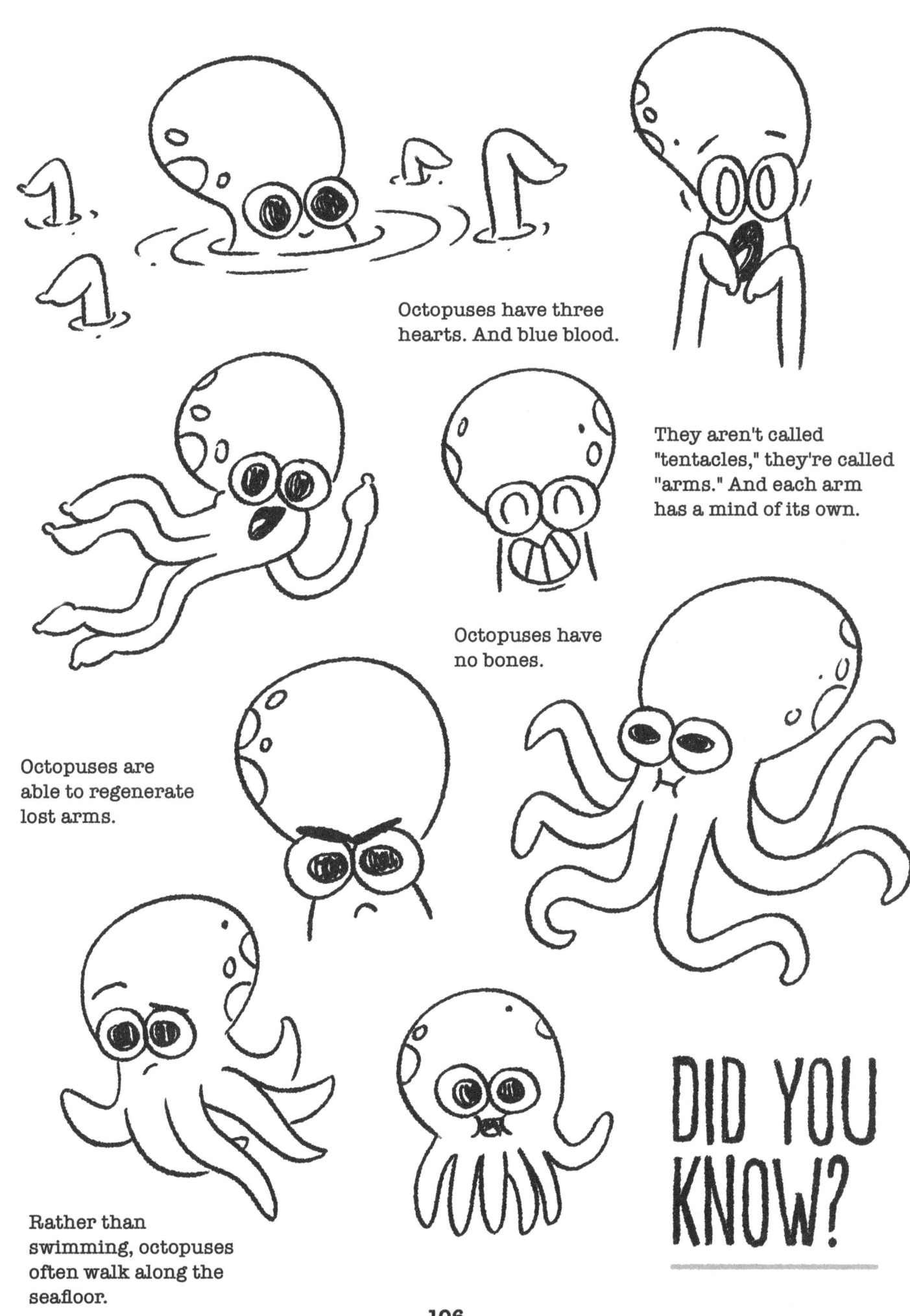

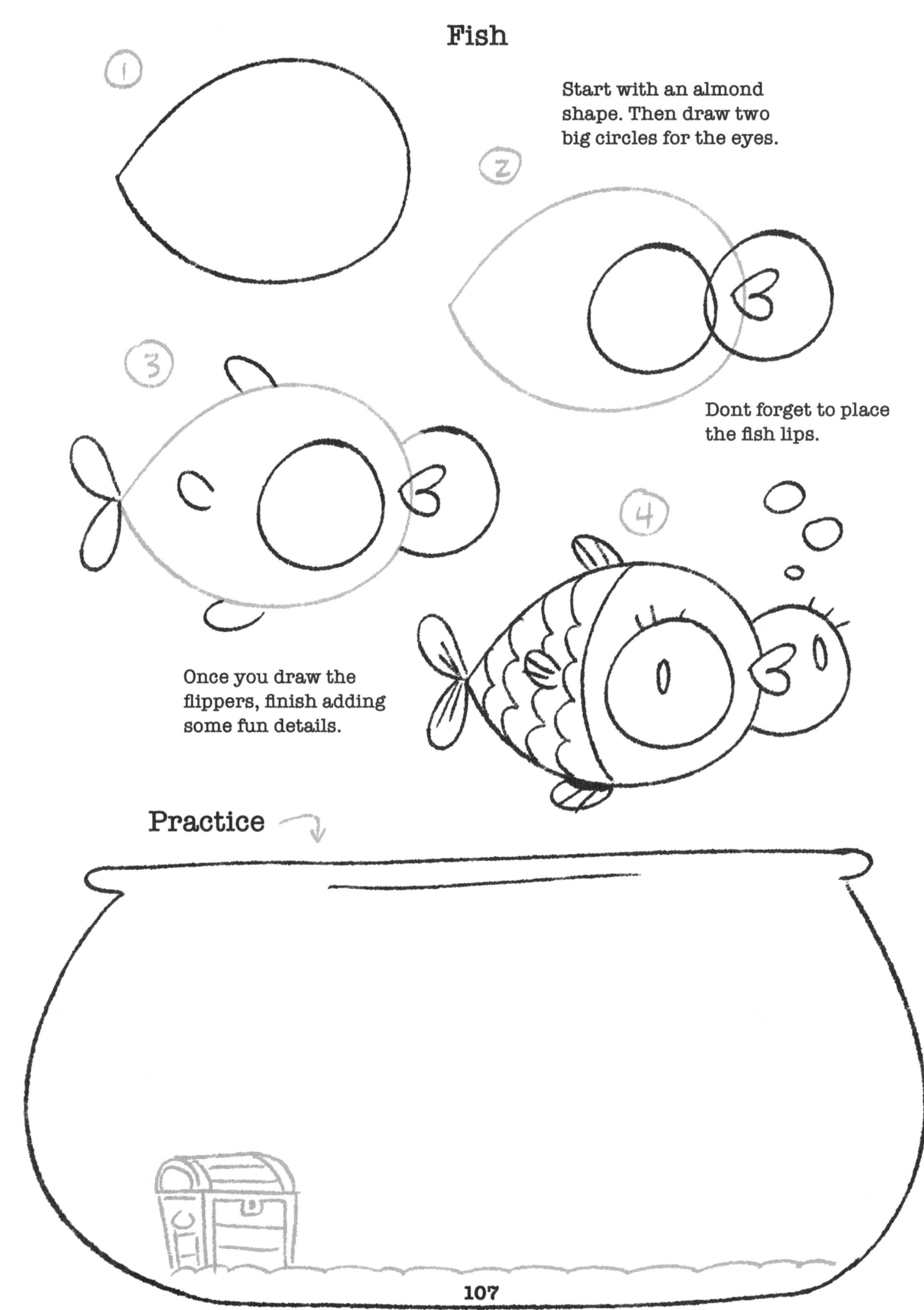

LEVEL UP!

When drawing cartoons, you have to push your initial drawing and exaggerate the features to be more silly!

REALISTIC

SIMPLIFIED

CARTOON

Practice

Shark

Follow the arrows when drawing the body.

Give it a big silly smile. Then you can add the fins

Don't forget the big teeth!

TIPS & TRICKS

Practice drawing a silly shark by following the grid on the left.

Use the grid to copy the shark drawing.

DID YOU KNOW?

Sharks can sense the presence of blood in the water.

There are more than 400 different types of sharks in the world, including the Great White shark, the Blue shark and the Mako. Every ocean in the world shares its space with some of these shark species.

DID YOU KNOW?

Starfish are not fish at all.

They do not swim, as fish do. Instead, they use their tube-like feet to slowly walk across the ocean floor.

This is why scientists often do not refer to them as 'fish' but as 'sea stars.'

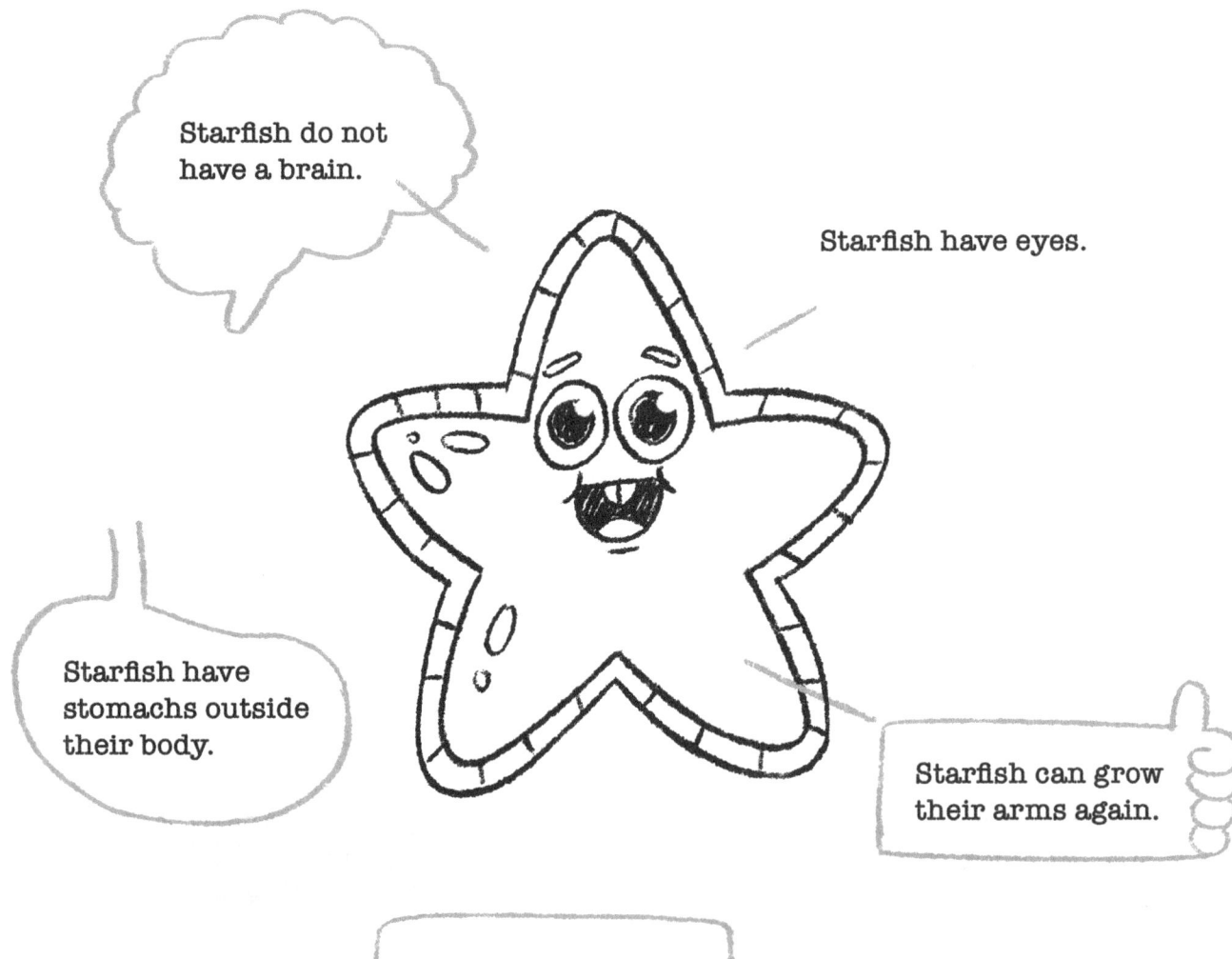

Starfish do not have a brain.

Starfish have eyes.

Starfish have stomachs outside their body.

Starfish can grow their arms again.

Starfish do not have any blood.

Practice
Give the stars some fun expressions.

Face ideas

Swordfish

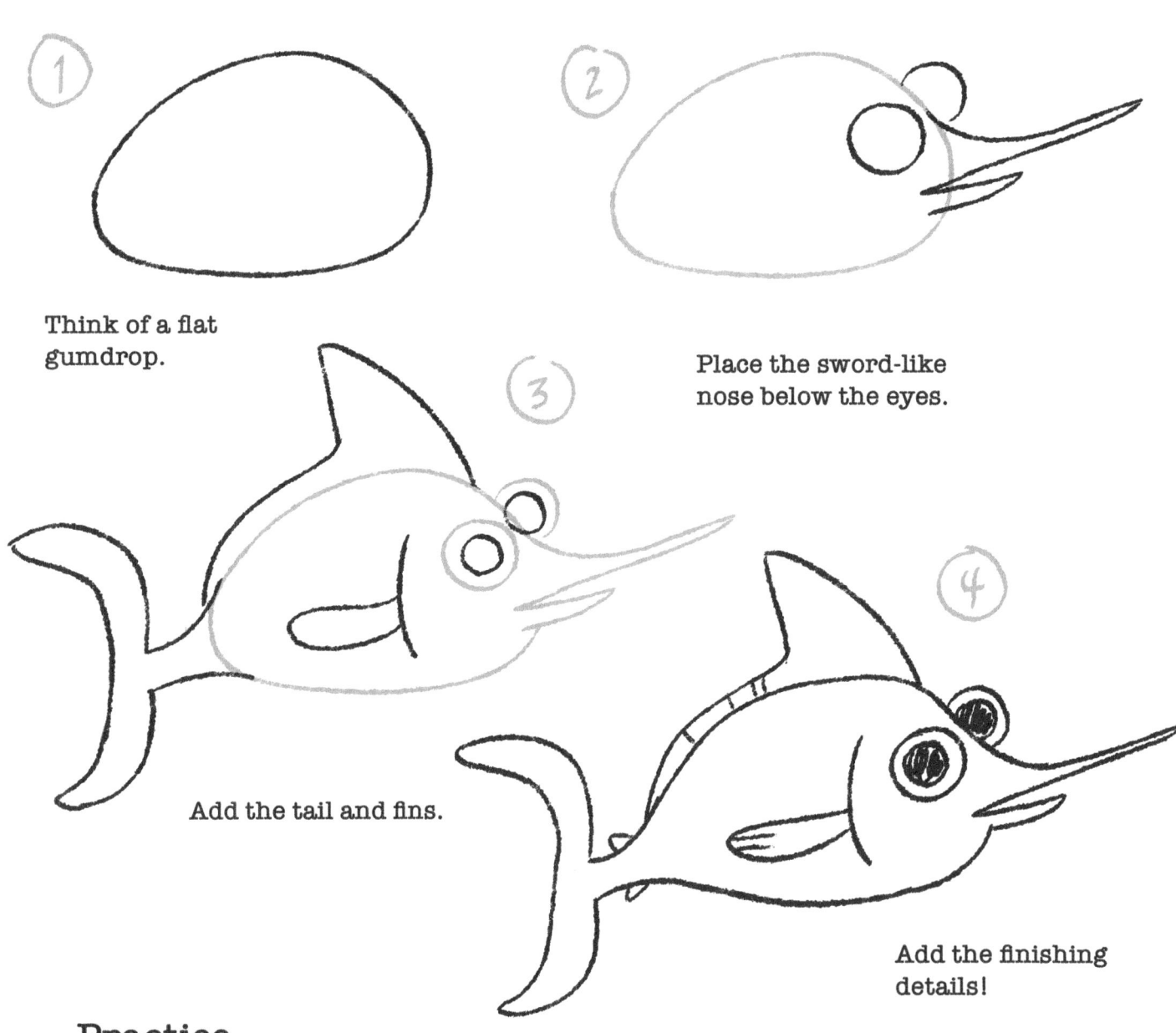

Think of a flat gumdrop.

Place the sword-like nose below the eyes.

Add the tail and fins.

Add the finishing details!

Practice

Narwhal

Start with a balloon top, followed by where the tail will be.

Add more details, like its horn and tail.

Don't forget a silly face to make it fun!

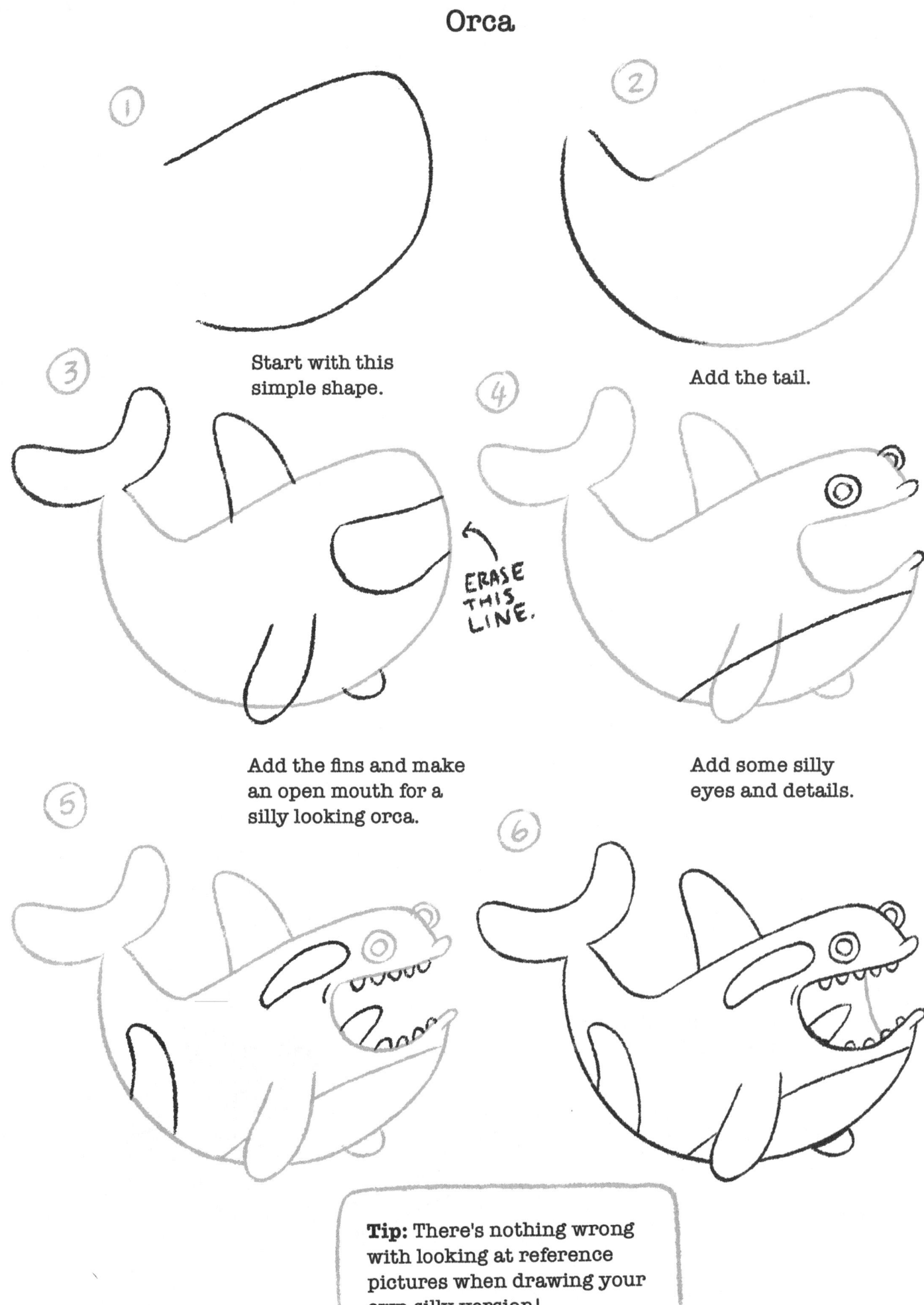

DID YOU KNOW?

Orcas are also known as killer whales.

Orcas live in small groups called pods.

Orcas are part of the dolphin family.

Orcas eat fish, squid, sea turtles, sharks, and other kinds of whales.

Orcas are called "wolves of the sea" because they travel and hunt in groups similar to wolves.

Practice

BARK & MEOW

CAT
DOG
BIRD
HAMSTER
SNAKE
MONKEY
PIG
TORTOISE
RABBIT
DOG

Learn how to draw these silly pets!

Cats

Cat

Draw a half circle for the head with a wider part at the bottom for cheeks.

Add a small "U" shape as the body.

Draw eyes and ears.

Draw the tail and body details.

Draw arms, legs, and all the final details!

Practice

Draw another kind of silly cat!

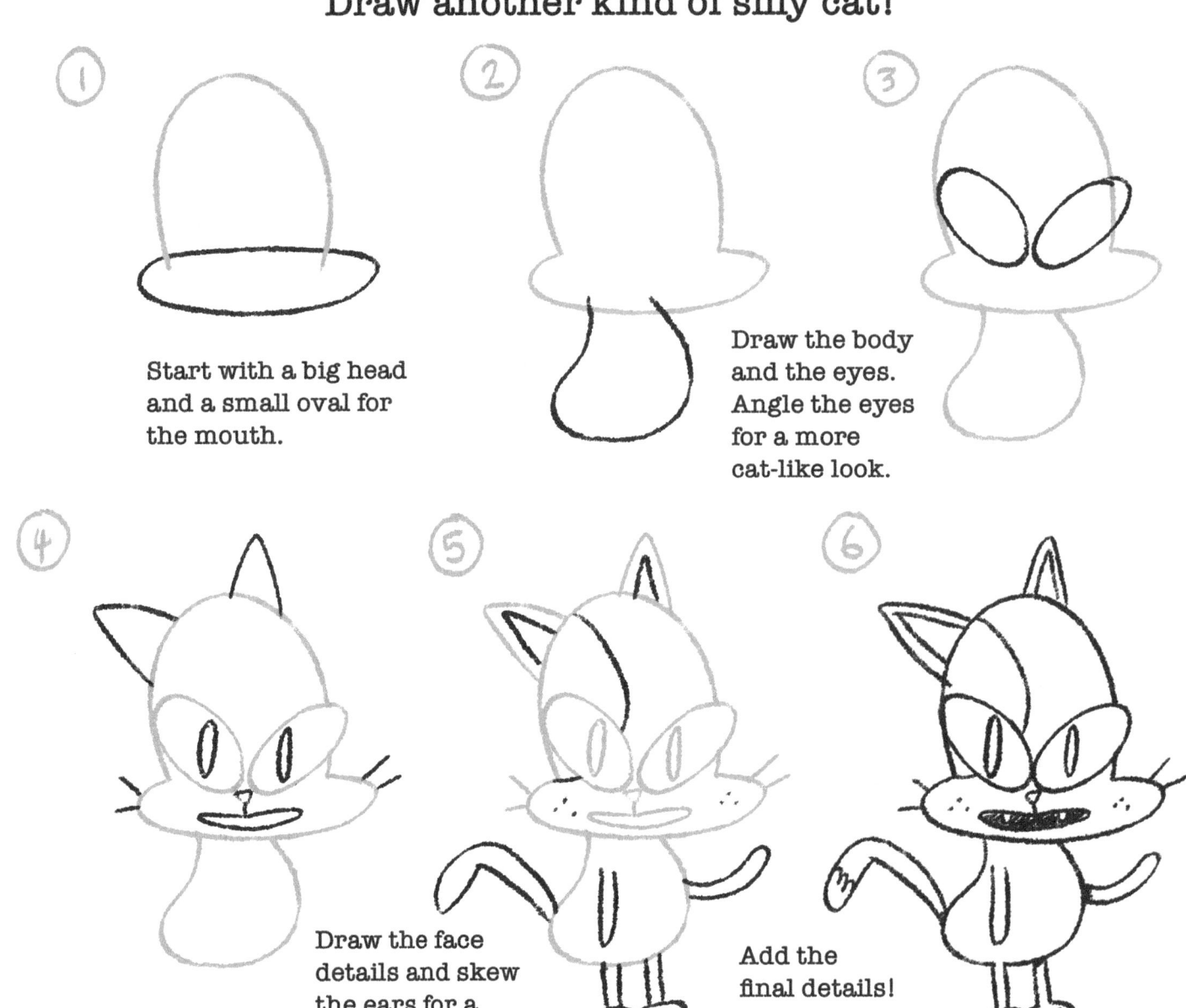

1. Start with a big head and a small oval for the mouth.
2. Draw the body and the eyes. Angle the eyes for a more cat-like look.
3.
4. Draw the face details and skew the ears for a sillier look.
5.
6. Add the final details!

Practice

Dogs

Chihuahua

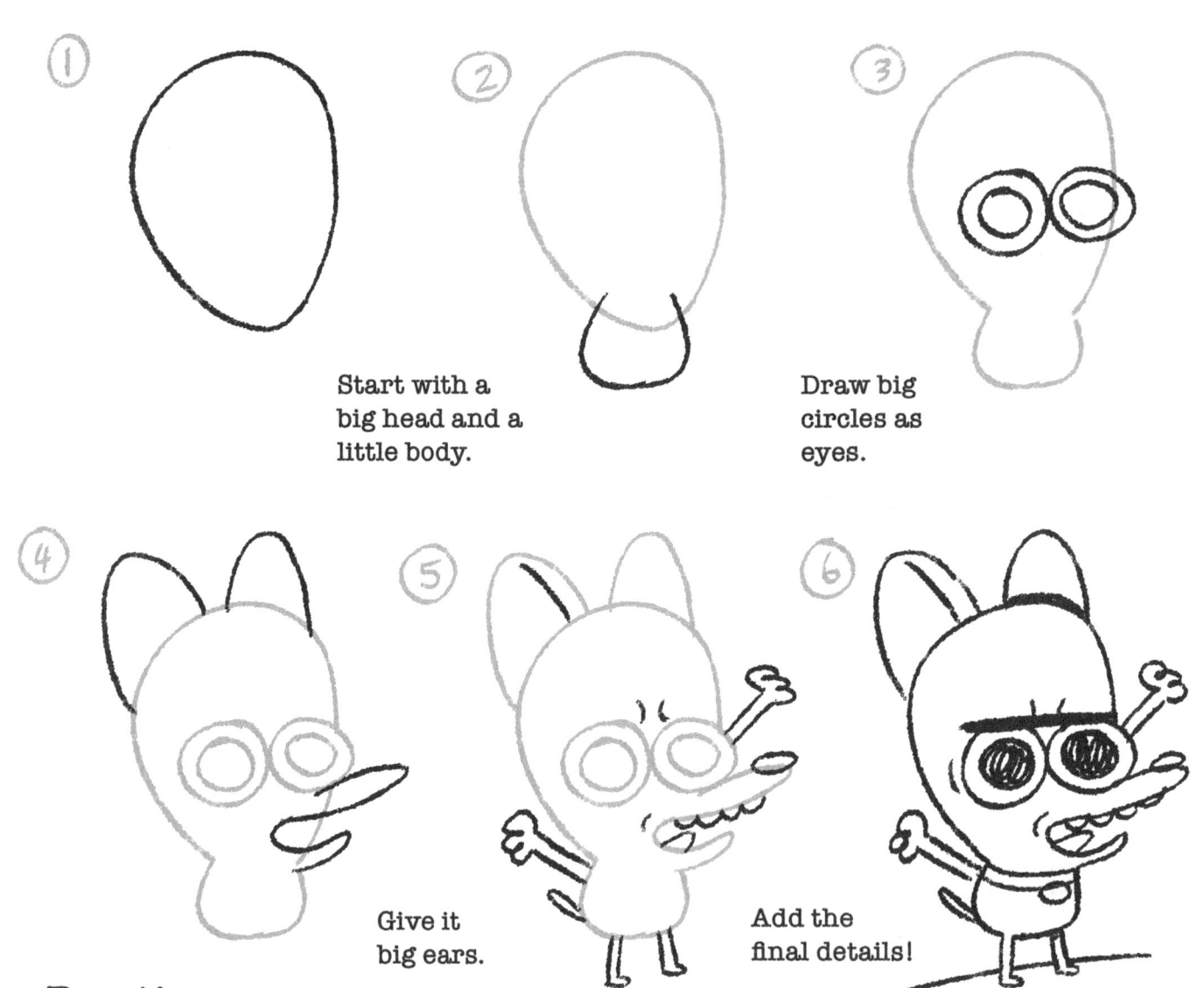

Practice

Draw a different kind of dog!

Having a big head with a tiny body is always fun!

Draw big eyes.

Give your dog silly eyes with a tongue hanging out for maximum silliness!

Practice

WHAT IS THE DOG THINKING ABOUT?

Bunny

Draw a rounded square with extra space for the jaw of the bunny. Then draw a smaller circle for the body.

After you connect the head to the body you can add the ears and the legs.

After you erase the extra lines, you can draw the face.

Don't forget the fluffy tail.

Now place the arms. Make it silly!

Make sure you finish all the fun details.

Pigeon

 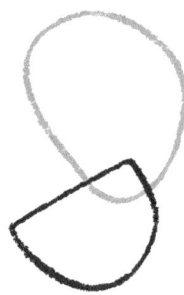

Start with two basic shapes for the head and body.

Erase the overlapping lines.

Add the beak and the neck plumage.

You can refine the wings and feet.

Add finishing details.

Practice

TURN THESE SHAPES INTO EXOTIC PETS

DRAW A CRAZY PET YOU'D LIKE TO HAVE

Hamster

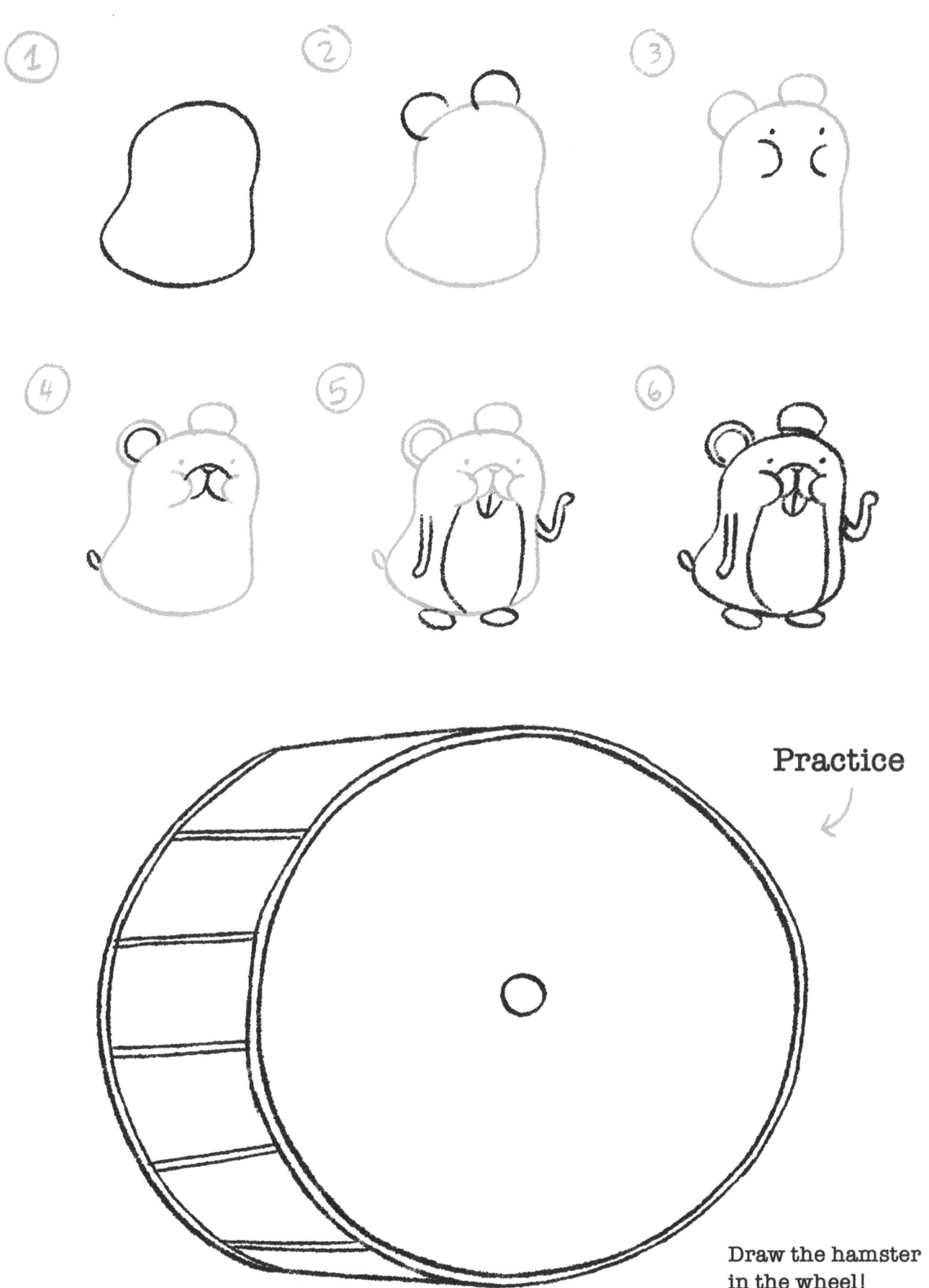

Practice

Draw the hamster in the wheel!

Monkey

DID YOU KNOW?

The main difference between a monkey and an ape is their tail. Monkeys have a tail, and apes do not.

Pig

Practice

Pigs do not sweat but regulate their body temperature in mud.

DID YOU KNOW?

Pigs are considered the smartest domesticated animals.

Pigs are among the most intelligent creatures on the earth.

LEVEL UP!

Level up by learning how to draw the cat sleeping.

①

②

③

④

Practice

LEVEL UP!

Make your character recognizable from a simple silhouette alone.

Exaggeration

→ PLAY WITH SHAPES THAT WILL MAKE YOUR CHARACTER LOOK SILLY.

Simple shape body

Snake

Practice

①

CONNECT ME

Did the snake get tangled?
Connect the snake however
you want!

Example

WHO DID I JUST EAT?

②

Draw one of the characters you learned in the snake's belly.

③ DRAW A FUN SNAKE PATTERN

Snakes have all sorts of fun patterns.
Can you come with a cool pattern?
You can also color it!

DID YOU KNOW?

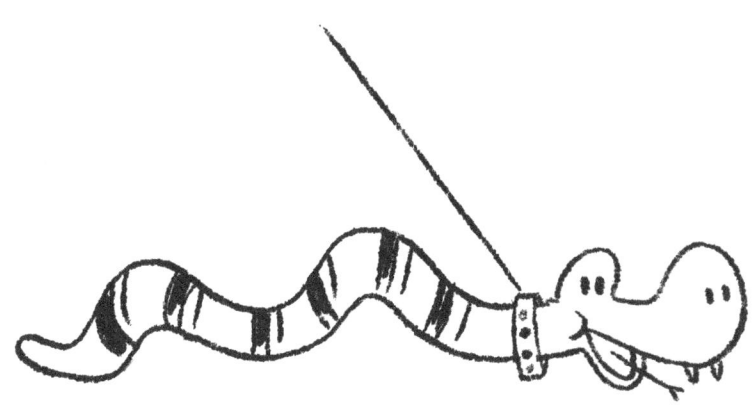

Snakes are becoming very popular pets. Over 500,000 households have snakes as pets in the United States.

Snakes cannot create body heat on their own.

The fastest snake in the world is the black mamba, which has been recorded at 12.5 miles per hour.

Reticulated pythons can reach 33 feet in length.

Tortoise

Draw the head as shown.

Make a wide "U" shape for the body.

Draw a silly face, and draw the neck hole.

Draw stubby arms and legs.

Draw stripes on the chest to represent the shell.

Finish adding all the details.

Practice

DID YOU KNOW?

All tortoises are turtles, but not all turtles are tortoises.

| Turtle | vs. | Tortoise |

Turtle	Tortoise
Turtles live or spend lots of time in water. Their shells are more flat, thin, and streamlined.	Tortoises live on land, and have rounded, dome-shaped shells.
Turtles shed their old scutes (external shell plates).	Tortoises don't shed anything from their shells.
Turtle feet are webbed with long claws, or even flippers.	Tortoises have feet that are padded and stumpy, like tiny elephant feet.
Turtles are omnivores.	Tortoises are primarily herbivores.
Turtles average 30 years. Sea turtles average 65 years.	Tortoises have an average lifespan of 90 years.

THE END

If you liked this book, and you want more characters and tutorials, join us at GENIUSCATBOOKS.COM for more fun content.

Join us on Instagram or Facebook @GENIUSCATBOOKS

If you purchased this book and you can leave a review, we really appreciate it if you'd give us your honest feedback!

 Genius Cat Books

Made in the USA
Monee, IL
12 December 2023

48924468R00079